Finding the Sanctuary Within

Reverend Mother Queen Almeta Rhonda Bowman

Copyright © 2007

By Rev. Almeta Rhonda Bowman
Library of Congress Control Number TX 1-576-447

All rights reserved. No part of this book may be reproduced or transmitted in any form or by any means without written permission from the author.

Scripture quotations from the Bible:
KJV- King James Version
NKJV- New King James Version
NIV- New International Version

ISBN 978-1546995296

Published in 2017

I LOVE YOU

TO: _____

FROM: _____

DATE: _____

OCCASION: _____

TABLE OF CONTENTS

Dedication 9
Acknowledgements 11
Foreword 12
Preface 13
Introduction 14
Opening Prayer 17

Chapter One - What is the Sanctuary 19

Chapter Two - The Journey 22

Chapter Three – A Sacred Place 31

Chapter Four - Entering and Locating the Sanctuary Within 36

Chapter Five - Our Secret Place 42

Chapter Six - Exploring the Sanctuary Within 48

Chapter Seven – Being in the Sanctuary Within 50

Chapter Eight - Healing In the Sanctuary 55

Chapter Nine - Pastors and Leaders 59

Chapter Ten - Emerging From the Sanctuary 66

Chapter Eleven - A New Person in Christ 69

Chapter Twelve - Receiving the Anointing Of the Holy Spirit 75

Chapter Thirteen - Sharing the Fruits, Gifts and Love of
the Holy Spirit with Others 78

Chapter Fourteen - The Gift of Love 81

Expressions of Love 89
Afterword 112
Closing Prayer 113
About Author 115
Journal 118
Daily Affirmations of the Scriptures 131

Finding the Sanctuary Within

DEDICATION

I first give all the praise, glory and honor to God. I thank Him for what He has done in my life; for the greater that is coming; and for the miracles He will perform in the lives of others. This book is dedicated in honor of my deceased mother, Gloria Estelle Bowman and my brothers Reginald and Stanley Bowman. To my family members: William Thomas Bowman, my father; Jovette Bowman-Dupree, Diane Bowman Jones, my sisters; Alpheus R. Bowman SR, Arthur L. Plummer Jr., Anwar A. Bowman SR, my sons; Rashida Bowman, Raven Plummer, my daughters-in-law; Justin, Teyara, Anwar Jr, Alpheus Jr, Devin, Audrianna, Zianna, Alexus, my grandchildren; and Jade, Justice, Amarae Leigh, my three great granddaughters, for their love and support.

SPECIAL THANKS

To My Editors Rose Carter and Aileen London, Graphic Designer Jaleel Hodges, Bishops, Elders, Pastors, Church Leaders, extended family, friends, associates, and faithful supporters, I thank God for the encouragement, knowledge, wisdom, patience and love that I have received from all of you. To everyone in the world who would love to have a closer more spirit filled life and experience with God. I hope you are blessed by these words of wisdom as well as this book.

And the Lord make you to increase and abound in love one toward another, and toward all men, even as we do toward you.
1 Thessalonians 3:12 KJV

PEACE, LOVE AND MANY BLESSINGS

I LOVE ALL OF YOU IN THE PRECIOUS, LOVING, PEACEFUL, SWEET, HEALING, FORGIVING, MIRACULOUS AND ON TIME NAME OF JESUS CHRIST

ACKNOWLEDGEMENTS

Many thanks to family members who said, "You can do it!" "Just go for it!" Bishop Glen Alonzo Staples was a great inspiration and blessing to my spirit. I also thank him for encouraging me to complete the many books that God has placed in my spirit; and for encouraging me to reach for higher heights. I thank God for leading me to The Temple of Praise on July 29, 2007. I prayed that God would place me where I would have the opportunity to praise and worship Him in spirit and truth.

Many thanks, to all who had the confidence in me and for supporting me on many levels. To all who are blessed after reading this book, know that when we humble ourselves, trust and have faith in God, The Holy Scriptures will reassure us that we can handle all the challenges that we may have to experience in this life. If God allows the challenges, it is because He has everything in Perfect Divine Order according to His Perfect Divine Will.

Please know that our struggle is over.

If the Son therefore shall make you free, ye shall be free indeed.
John 8:36 KJV

Now the Lord is that Spirit; where the Spirit of the Lord is, there is liberty.
2 Corinthians 3:17 KJV

FOREWORD

Years ago, Reverend Almeta Rhonda Bowman realized a hope that God had placed in her heart to reach His people. When God released Reverend Bowman to write her very first book, He opened the doors of Heaven and poured out a blessing that she didn't have room enough to receive. She then took her plentiful harvest and shared what God had given her in this book, "Finding The Sanctuary Within."

When my wife and I were asked by Reverend Bowman to write her Foreword it was a privilege. She has truly been a blessing to many. We thank God for her willingness to serve. No matter what the task, Reverend Bowman has always been in position to pray. She is a prayer warrior on the battlefield for the Lord. Reverend Bowman unlocked extraordinary power in the Word of God which exemplified what she experienced and who she is in the Body of CHRIST. In her book, you will feel the love of CHRIST and a whole lot of what God has to offer according to the good works of His people.

We pray this book will reach millions so that they may reap the harvest God put in place for Reverend Bowman to deliver. We also pray that this book serve as an avenue to open up the eyes of many, lead the unsaved to the foot of the cross and remind those who are already saved to remain at the foot of the cross.

Bishop Thomas G. Winborne Sr.
&
First Lady Jackie Winborne
GOT Deliverance Ministry
Capital Heights Md
20743

PREFACE

This book is a spiritual and inspirational guide to living a more productive and spirit filled life. I pray this book will reach people who have experienced conditions that were life altering. Conditions such as medical issues, drugs, loneliness, feelings of inadequacy, betrayal in love, incarceration and death. This book will be a great inspirational read for parents, teachers, social workers, pastors, church leaders, and students. The heart that finds the sanctuary within will be reconstructed by God to develop spiritual wings to soar like an eagle.

But they that wait upon the Lord shall renew their strength; they shall mount up with wings as eagles; they shall run, and not be weary; and they shall walk and not faint.
Isaiah 40:31 KJV

INTRODUCTION

As a product of a strict Pentecostal family, I was raised under the leadership of my parents William and Gloria Bowman. My father is deacon in the church and my mother was a missionary. Daily bible study, learning the infallible Word of God and participation in church activities was a way of life for me. I was taught to love, and extend kindness to everyone. My mother's motto was "Don't treat people the way they treat you, treat them the way you would want to be treated." Growing up, I could never understand her motto, but over the years, her words continued to resonate in my spirit. Through experience and the manifold wisdom of God, I now understand what my mother was saying. I have been spiritually blessed, anointed and appointed by God to be a blessing to His people. My assignments are to encourage God's people, extend unconditional love to them, and feed them with the life changing infallible Word of God. I pray that this book will plant an abundance of our God's seeds of love, joy, peace, hope, wisdom, knowledge and understanding into the hearts of all His precious people. My brothers and sisters, as I humbly plant these seeds of wisdom, the Holy Spirit will water them. In His appointed time, God shall give the increase, bringing into fruition the fruits of the spirit which are:

Love, joy, peace, forbearance, kindness, goodness, faithfulness, gentleness and self-control to all who believe.
Galatians 5:22 KJV

At this appointed time in my life The Holy Spirit inspired me to write "Finding the Sanctuary Within." The revelation of "Finding the Sanctuary Within" will bless you and many generations to come in your family. Former trials, tribulations, situations and circumstances I encountered in this world could have made me an excellent candidate to give up on life. But by the grace of God, I am another miracle performed by God.

The Sanctuary Within is a place where God is always welcome. It is the space between each breath, the silence between each heartbeat and the stillness that is necessary for us to feel God's Divine Power. The Sanctuary Within is that sacred place within us, where no one may enter but The Spirit of God.

IS THERE ROOM FOR GOD IN MY LIFE?

In All Thy Ways Acknowledge Him And He Shall Direct Thy Path.
Proverbs 3:6 KJV

When we enter The Sanctuary Within we must repent of our sins, including the unknown sins disguised as mere mistakes. The act of honesty with ourselves as well as others will set us free, as we release our concerns, issues, uncontrollable situations and circumstances to God. We must trust Him, surrender our will, and allow God to heal and cleanse our inner sanctuary. By doing so, this will allow us to recognize the Spirit of God within us. We are created in the image and likeness of God, but the fall of man caused a great separation between God and man. Man therefore lost the supernatural experience of God's presence. The world around us is a distraction. That is why it is mandatory for us to retreat from this cruel and distracting world so that we may be quiet enough to hear God. As we enter The Sanctuary Within, please begin with a prayer to ask God for His forgiveness and to bless us with whatever He deems necessary. The Sanctuary Within blesses and allows us to experience the presence, joy, peace and love of God by transforming man's fallible character to mimic the infinite character of God. It is a place where we desperately hunger and thirst longing to receive God's promise. When God instructs us to be still it is because He is moving. If we are moving at the same time as God, a collision can cause us to miss our Divine Blessings.

Be still, and know that I am God.
Psalm 46:10 KJV

For a few moments, quiet your spirits and inhale the anointed breaths of God through your nose, slowly exhaling from your mouth. Repeat this eight times before we journey further toward "Finding The Sanctuary Within." We must permit The Divine Spirit of God to flow through us like a refreshing spring of water. As we enter into God's Palace, before His Divine Presence, we must totally empty ourselves in order to be filled with The Divine Holy Spirit and receive His Divine Glory. God, we truly desire to be consumed with Your Divine Anointing, Strength and Power for the rest of our lives in the Supplying name of Jesus. As we take the time to go within our sanctuaries, we will discover many God given treasures that only He can nurture. The Sanctuary Within is the dwelling place of God inside of us, where He is always waiting anticipating the time for us to receive Him.

Come unto me, all ye who labor and are heavy laden, and I will give you rest.
Matthew 11:28 KJV

OPENING PRAYER

Gracious Heavenly Father, we come before You in prayer with grateful and humble hearts in the wonderful and powerful name of Jesus. This is the day that the Lord has made we shall rejoice and be glad in it. Oh taste and see that the Lord is good and His mercy endureth forever. God, first, we are asking You to forgive sins we have committed by thought, word or deed and renew in us a clean heart fit for Your service. We are so thankful that you considered us to be a part of this Royal God given day. We are also thankful to you for keeping all of our love ones as well. Father God it is truly a pleasure on this day, to unconditionally love everyone You allow to cross our paths. We will with great joy give Your name all the praise, glory and honor. Father God as we continue to gracefully move forward in this day, please open our hearts and minds so that we may experience and receive the many blessings and golden nuggets this book has to offer. Father God we thank You so much for Your unconditional love and many acts of kindness. Father God, we want to embrace You on a whole new level in our spirits. If there is anything in us that is not like You, we ask You to remove in the cleansing name of Jesus. We rebuke any demonic force that tries to hinder or block anything that needs to come forth from you. We thank you so much for the wonderful blessings we have received and we thank You in advance for the miraculous blessings we have yet to receive. We claim victory in the mighty name of Jesus knowing that no weapon formed against us shall prosper. Greater is He that is in me than he that is in the world. Father God we will continue to let our light shine so that others may find their way out of darkness. Father God when we come out of this prayer please bless us with a renewed mind and heart that is filled with Your unconditional love so that we may run on and see what the end is going to be. Father God we thank You so much for hearing and answering our prayers according to Your Divine Will, Time, Purpose And Order for The Destiny of our lives in the sweet, loving, healing, forgiving, on time and miraculous name of Jesus. Amen

CHAPTER ONE

WHAT IS THE SANCTUARY?

S-Sacred Safe Place
A-Anointed Because Of God
N-Never Ending
C-Center of Our Being That Balances Us
T-The Tabernacle and the Truth
U-Unites the Spirit of God's
A-Awareness
R-Reconstruction and Restoration Within
Y-You

We are a blessed people to have a sacred and safe place within our hearts called "The Sanctuary Within". "The Sanctuary Within" has been anointed by God. No other spirits may enter only The Spirit of God is welcomed. God has anointed that space so that never ending blessings can flow. It is the space between each breath, the silence between each heartbeat and the stillness that's necessary for us to feel God's Divine Presence and Power. "The Sanctuary Within" is the center of our being. We become balanced, because the truth of God unites spiritual awareness within us. We are being reconstructed and restored from within.

Are We Really Leaving Room For The Holy Spirit?
Do We Acknowledge or Even Recognize Our God's Presence?

Most often the answer to both of these questions is no. We are so preoccupied with the things of the world that we have become distracted from recognizing when we are in the midst of His Presence. Many of our actions show that we are operating from negative forces which we think are natural. We have been stuck in a carnal state of thinking for far too long. We have allowed too many negative outside influences to control and contaminate our mind, soul and spirit.

Our Bodies Are The Temple Of God. We Must Allow The Spirit And Word Of God To Cleanse Us And Put Us Back On The Right Track.

Do you know that we are the temple of God and that the spirit of God dwells in us? If any man defile the temple of God, him shall God destroy; for the temple of God is Holy, which temple ye are.
1 Corinthians 3:16-17 NKJV

Now he who searches the hearts knows what the mind of the spirit is, because he makes intercession for the saints according to the will of God.
Romans 8:27 NKJV

Let us draw near with a true heart in full assurance of faith, having our hearts sprinkled from an evil conscience, and our bodies washed with pure water.
Hebrews 10:22 NKJV

Scripture also tells us to be careful what we utter from our mouths.
Death and life are in the power of the tongue and those who love it will eat its fruit.
Proverbs 18:21 NKJV

The importance of Finding the Sanctuary Within is to know our self-worth, and acknowledge our strengths and weakness so that we may be truly humbled and become more Christ like. We need to admit that we need God because knowing Him personally is essential to our well-being. By God's grace and mercy, each breath we take renews a powerful life force within us. Let us be grateful and thankful for the very breath and spirit that dwells within us this very moment. The next breath does not belong to us, it belongs to God.

Our spirit must be totally receptive in order for us to hear God clearly. As we are Finding The Sanctuary Within, our goal should be to empty ourselves of all negativity so that we are able to come out of our dark state of mind and be victorious. We will then be able to receive the goodness and blessings of our God. As a result, we will be blessed with a mind that produces positive thinking.

FOOD FOR THOUGHT

I find that we take better care of our tangible things than we do our mind, body and soul. Please remember to reflect on what our minds think and the words that are absorbed in our spirit.

For they that are after the flesh do mind the things of the flesh; but they that are after the spirit the things of the spirit.
Romans 8:5 KJV

The world around us distracts us and that is why we must retreat from the world so that we may be quiet and hear God.

CHAPTER TWO

THE JOURNEY TOWARDS FINDING THE SANCTUARY WITHIN

As we journey toward experiencing The Sanctuary Within, we must have complete faith, and trust. We acknowledge that we must wait on God to make the difference in our lives because His Timing is Perfect. It is time to surrender our nasty, wicked and hateful ways and allow God to step into the doorway of our heart, set up residence, change, rearrange and prepare us for His Divine Glory. In all of this, please remember that The Sanctuary Within is a very sacred space that affords us the great pleasure of humbly submitting our prayers and supplication's unto God, allowing Him to remove anything that is not like Him. We must be open enough so that God can fill all the voids and emptiness we may experience. My brothers and sisters, please know that even though we put our faith and trust in God, on this life's journey we will encounter many fiery darts. These fiery darts manifest themselves in the form of adversity. But, all thanks are to God, that through Christ we are able to quench those fiery darts. Using the schemes and plans devised by the adversary, God strengthens us as He continues to reveal His Unconditional Love and Divine Grace.

Finally, my brethren, be strong in the Lord, and in the power of His might. Put on the whole armor of God that ye may be able to stand against the wiles of the devil. For we wrestle not against flesh and blood, but against principalities, against powers, against the rulers of the darkness of this world, against spiritual wickedness in high places.

Wherefore, take unto you the whole armor of God that ye may be able to withstand in the evil day, and having done all, to stand. Stand therefore, having your loins girt about with truth, and having on the breastplate of righteousness; and your feet shod with the preparation of the gospel of peace; above all, taking the shield of faith, wherewith ye shall be able to quench all the fiery darts of
the wicked.

And take the helmet of salvation, and the sword of the spirit, which is the word of God praying always with all prayer and supplication in the spirit, and watching thereunto with all perseverance and supplication for all saints.
Ephesians 6:10-18 KJV

My precious brothers and sisters, when God chooses us for the journey and sends us out on the battlefield, He anoints, provides and equips us with everything necessary. Through deception the devil, who is the wicked one, conspires and manipulates the minds of unsuspecting souls with his principalities, rulers of darkness and spiritual wickedness in high places. For this cause, we must be cautious and remember that we wrestle not against flesh and blood. It is dangerous and unwise to attempt to fight Satan and his hordes on our own. The only way possible is to trust, have faith in the Power of God that we will prevail in the awesome Name of Jesus Christ. The Sanctuary Within is that place where we can pray and ask God for whatever we need as long as it is according to His Perfect Divine Will. This book is designed for everyone who seeks a closer walk and relationship with God and for those who have the awesome task of nurturing the souls and spirit of all of Gods precious people.

And we know that all things work together for good to them that love God, to them who are the called according to his purpose.
Romans 8:28 KJV

Daily life imposed depression, oppression, and rejection over my life, causing delay in the birth of Finding the Sanctuary Within. Episodes of sciatic nerve pain imposed on me a stillness that brought me to the realization that God allows pain in our lives so that He can have our undivided attention.

My People Are Destroyed For the Lack of Knowledge.
Hosea 4:6 (KJV)

I can truly say that God has blessed, anointed and prepared me to be a blessing for the empowerment of others. God had freed me to share part of my story about how He has kept me through the many adversities in my life. We all have our own cross-to bear and our own stories to tell. My story includes many years of mental and physical abuse. I began thinking about my past and remembered that at the young age of thirteen I had a traumatic experience outside of the home that caused a mental and spiritual disconnect for me causing me to be very numb for a very long time. My story masks excruciating pain, taking of prescription and non-prescription narcotics and constant visits to the emergency rooms and doctor's office. None of those things were really cures. They were not helping me to heal or get better. Those drugs caused me to hallucinate, accomplish very little, experience dysfunctional communication, all of which affected my day to day living. Those pills and drugs could have caused serious damage to my health with prolong usage. Many of us, in some form or fashion, mask our pain. Masking our pain is only a temporary cover up so that we don't have to deal with it. Masking the pain only delays our healing process. If we're not dealing with the root cause of the problems, we are just delaying the inevitable resurfacing of the pain. This is why it is so important to remove those masks and deal with the source or root cause of our pain and issues that include:

- Rejection
- Un-forgiveness
- Bitterness
- Loneliness
- Hatefulness
- Feeling Inadequate
- Unloved
- Uncertain
- Insecure
- Betrayed
- Violated
- And Fear In Our Hearts

The list can go on and on; you fill in the blanks as it applies to you. It has been a slow process to recovery for me, yet a blessing in disguise.

God has given me valuable time to reevaluate a lot of things and to put them in their proper perspective. One of the greatest things for me is to see my book about Finding the Sanctuary Within being typed by my hands. While writing this book, I could hear my mother saying to me, Almeta, you have the patience of Job. My brothers and sisters, please allow me to share this book with you; through all that I have been through, our God has developed in me an even greater measure of faith, patience and appreciation of Who He really is to me in the name of Jesus. Life experiences have really made it possible for me to truly understand what my mother meant. I also know that I am being prepared for something far greater than just writing books. Please know that because we claim the name of Jesus, we will experience setbacks, sit-downs, and even some turn arounds as we journey toward the straight and narrow way of life and Finding The Sanctuary Within.

Today, I truly thank God for my parent's teachings and Christian upbringing that taught, comforted and allowed me to search my soul. I realized that I had to trust, have faith and believe in God all over again. Maybe this sounds familiar and you can relate to this statement. I am also sick and tired of the games that I have allowed people to play with my life. I am so grateful to God for keeping me through all of the hurt, pain and discouragements in the miraculous name of Jesus.

I now have a clearer understanding that it was only a test and part of the process of stepping in to new levels. God was preparing and strengthening me for my future destiny. I realized that people cannot define who you are, especially in Christ, God has already done that.

That evil spirit thought he had won in the quest to destroy my mind so that this book, as well as many others, would not come forward. But I truly thank God for His Divine Healing, Keeping and Protecting Power in the Miraculous Name of Jesus. As long as there is breath in this body, I shall serve God with my whole heart and for all the right reasons. The time spent being still in The Sanctuary Within has helped me to deal with myself and forgive those related to my past. God has blessed me with the wisdom of knowing that unconditional love is the key in spite of what we may go through. The Bible teaches us that our great example of unconditional love is our Father God, His Son and our Savior Jesus Christ.

For God so loved the world, that he gave his only begotten Son, that whosoever believeth in him should not perish, but have everlasting life. For God sent not his Son into the world to condemn the world; but that the world through him might be saved.
John 3:16-17 KJV

So at this very second I asked God to bestow His Healing and Forgiving Power upon us all.

God, I pray that this book will help all readers and hearers to look back over their lives and know that You have kept and brought us all a mighty long way. Moving forward toward Finding the Sanctuary Within will give us all a greater appreciation of God's Unconditional Love, Joy, Peace and Happiness. The Sanctuary Within is in our hearts where The Spirit of The True and Living God lives. Our God is very powerful; we must give Him the royal opportunity to manifest Himself in our lives in greater magnitude. We will face challenges, test, trails, and tribulation on our journey, some caused by others, some of our own doings and some ordained by God. Once upon a time, I thought I would not make it, but through it all, I am here, a strong miracle of God and full of His Unconditional Love, with a Humble and Forgiving heart.

For God teaches us that:

I can do all things through Christ which strengthens me.
Philippians 4:13

My brothers and sisters, here are some questions we must ask ourselves:

- *Is God truly a part of my life?*

- *If He isn't a part of our lives then what are we substituting for God?*

- *We all need to be inspired, so what is my inspiration?*

- *Why do we choose to enter spaces of chaos and confusion that cause havoc in our minds and lives?*

- *Why do we keep allowing unpleasant spirits in our space?*

We, as a people, have become accustomed and comfortable with accepting anyone, or anything just to belong. We need to know that those unwanted spirits only block the entrance to truly Finding The Sanctuary Within and living a more fruitful, productive and spirit-filled life.

For though we walk in the flesh, we do not war after the flesh: For the weapons of our warfare are not carnal, but mighty through God to the pulling down of strong holds; Casting down imaginations and every high thing that exalted itself against the knowledge of God, and bringing into captivity every thought to the obedience of Christ.
2 Corinthians 10:3-5 KJV

Here we must prepare our inner being to receive what God has to offer us. The Sanctuary Within is a place we make room for God in our lives and there are no distractions there.

But seek ye first the kingdom of God, and his righteousness; and all these things shall be added unto you.
Matthew 6:33 KJV

The beautiful part about being in The Sanctuary Within is that God begins a reconstruction in our minds, hearts and souls. The Spirit of God begins to tear down the walls, and barriers that had been built up for many years. Those walls and barriers have hindered us from moving forward to our Divine Destinies. Here's an awesome news flash: "We serve a God who is able to get to the root of all our problems that have caused us to have such weak minds, hateful and unforgiving hearts." In The Sanctuary Within, God blesses us to have a renewed mind, heart and spirit that is transformed to enlighten this generation and generations to come. Again I say, "Are we really making room or taking the time for our God to manifest Himself to us?"

IS THERE ROOM FOR GOD IN MY LIFE?

The Sanctuary Within is the place where God is always welcome. It is the space between each breath, the silence between each heart beat and the stillness that necessary for us to know His Divine Presence and Power. My brothers and sisters please embrace that stillness for it is a serene place of receiving the Miraculous Anointing of our God.

PRAYER

God, I come before you right now with a humble and sincere heart asking you to move on the hearts and minds of all your sons and daughters who welcome and desire a Divine change in their lives. Please renew a right spirit in all of us. Prepare us to honor, praise and adore You. God we are in great expectation to experience Your Divine Touch and to receive that brighter light which will shine upon our path as well as others. In advance, God we receive Your Divine Direction and instructions for our lives. Please continue to anoint us with fresh Divine Revelation, about what it means to be in your Divine Presence. God we thank you for being our Strong Tower; our Joy, and our Peace. God, I now ask You to take full control of our total being so that You may bless us with a peace that surpasses all understanding in the matchless, powerful and awesome name of Jesus Christ. Amen!

CHAPTER THREE

A SACRED PLACE

The Sanctuary Within is a very sacred place where we are ready, willing, and able to receive God on a whole new level and experience. Now that we have acknowledged God in our sacred place, He will reveal Himself and our true identity to us. It is vital that we know who we are in Christ so that we may live and be effective in His kingdom here on earth. The Sanctuary Within is that sacred dwelling place of God within us. While in The Sanctuary Within, our God begins to uproot all those seeds of hatefulness, meanness, arrogance, controlling and jealous spirits, as well as unforgiving hearts. Whatever negative spirits you may have, just add them to the list.

We must allow our God to plant His Divine Seeds of Love, Joy and Peace into our hearts. We need all of these vital ingredients on a daily basis. These God given seeds will enrich our minds; give us soft hearts and sweet spirits to prepare us to live more effective and fruitful lives. These Anointed seeds are from God, when we receive them, God's Divine Love and Healing Power can flow through our lives freely. We are now able to commune, connect, and find all of the creativity that we have been truly blessed with. Finding The Sanctuary Within and being in that sacred space also allows us to experience the True Character and Presence of our God.

And God said; Let us make man in our image, after our likeness: and let them have dominion over the fish of the sea, and over the fowl of the air,

and over the cattle, and over all the earth, and over every creeping thing that creepeth upon the earth.
Genesis 1:26 KJV

Our God thought of us and included us in His original plan before the beginning of time. For those who take the time to go within, know that our God shall reveal a lot of things to us about ourselves. We are just like seeds, when the right seeds are planted and nourished properly, they will take root and grow into something very beautiful. When we take the time to go within we experience God planting His Divine Seeds in us. The Holy Spirit will then use Living Water to nurture them. We may not see the change right away, so believe, have patience, have faith, and put our total trust in God during the growing process. In time we shall grow and blossom into beautiful and magnificent human beings, as we were designed to be from the beginning.

There must be continuous daily reading of the Word of God. Daily reading of the Word is essential because it enables us to receive great strength and power so that we do not get lost during the process. Others will become influenced and want to accept the ways and teachings of our God. For some, it may be a little uncomfortable at first to open up and share their personal feelings because they have suppressed them for so long. Please feel secure because as my Bishop Staples always says, "Our God is a Gentle Man and He also has that She Kind of Glory." Our God is all that and more.

Let us reflect on the Children of Israel. They entered the wilderness and wandered around for 40 years. It should have only taken them about 11 days to reach the promise land. We can all say that at some point and time in our lives we too have had some wilderness experiences that made us feel vulnerable, alone, and unprotected. And because of that, the evil spirit begins his attack, thereby, making us feel that God is nowhere near us during this process. Please allow me to share with you that nothing happens in our lives without God's approval. God allowed the children of Israel to wander around in circles because they were disobedient, headstrong, treacherous, disloyal, wicked, and arrogant people who complained continuously and were never satisfied for the great things our God made possible for them. Somewhat like us today. The Word of our God says:

Unto a land flowing with milk and honey; for I will not go up in the midst of thee; for thou art a stiff-necked people; lest I consume thee in the way.
Exodus 33:3

When we act out of character being mean, nasty, and wicked, we are rebelling against The Lord our God. We too shall be considered as The Disobedient Children of Israel.

Remember, and forget not, how thou provokedst the LORD thy God to wrath in the wilderness: from the day that thou didst depart out of the land of Egypt, until ye came unto this place, ye have been rebellious against the LORD.
Deuteronomy 9:7 KJV

Ye have been rebellious against the Lord from the day that I knew you. Thus I fell down before the Lord forty days and forty nights, as I fell down at the first; because the Lord had said he would destroy you. I prayed therefore unto the Lord, and said, O Lord God, destroy not thy people and thine inheritance, which thou hast redeemed through thy greatness, which thou hast brought forth out of Egypt with a mighty

hand. Remember thy servants, Abraham, Isaac, and Jacob; look not unto the stubbornness of this people, nor to their wickedness, nor to their sin:
Deuteronomy 9: 24-27 KJV

For the children of Israel walked forty years in the wilderness, till all the people that were men of war, which came out of Egypt, were consumed, because they obeyed not the voice of the Lord: unto whom the Lord sware that he would not shew them the land, which the Lord sware unto their fathers that he would give us, a land that floweth with milk and honey.
Joshua 5:6 KJV

Divine transformation and the reconstruction of their minds had to take place in the wilderness, so it is with us. That wilderness experience was apparently necessary for the children of Israel. God was preparing them to come out of the wilderness of their minds as a better people with many lessons learned as He will do for us as well. It doesn't have to be hard for us, because no matter what we go through, when God is in the equation, everything will be alright. All we must do is just listen to God and follow His Divine Instructions; it will make all the difference in the world.

My sheep hear my voice, and I know them, and they follow me.
John 10:27 KJV

If we expect our God to bless us, we must be obedient, faithful, grateful, serve Him with our whole heart, and be content with what we have, until He makes the Divine Change for and in our lives.

Let your conversation be without covetousness; and be content with such things as ye have: for he hath said, I will never leave thee, nor forsake thee.
Hebrews 13:5 KJV

Let us stop acting like the disobedient Children of Israel, be patient and thankful enough that our God would even consider and allow us to learn from our mistakes.

But Israel shall be saved in the LORD with an everlasting salvation: ye shall not be neither ashamed nor confounded world without end.
Isaiah 45:17 KJV

My brothers and sisters, because our God is so loving and kind, He has forgiven us on all levels and is ready and capable of restoring back to us everything we need in the mighty name of Jesus.

Who is a God like unto thee that pardoneth iniquity and passeth by the transgression of the remnant of His heritage? He retaineth not His anger forever, because He delighteth in mercy.
Micah 7:18 KJV

Please remember that if God parted the Red Sea for The Children of Israel, He will surely part the Red Sea in our lives as well. Our Red Sea can be deliverance from a corrupt way of thinking and doing things to a well-balanced mindset and life style of Jesus Christ.

CHAPTER FOUR

ENTERING AND LOCATING THE SANCTUARY WITHIN

He that dwelleth in the secret place of the most high shall abide under the shadows of the almighty.
Psalm 91:1

When I entered The Sanctuary Within, my heart and spirit were broken. I felt like a slave to society. Every time I drove past the George Washington Plantation in Mount Vernon, Virginia, I thought of slavery times. Sometimes I stopped there, got out and look at the trees. I would say to myself, if these trees could talk, I know they would have a story to tell about physical lynching. Some of us today are still being lynched, not in a physical sense of hanging on trees, but, our hearts and minds are being lynched and destroyed. Sometimes I felt as though I had been hung up and lynched. I realized that I was hung up in my own mind, because of all the hurt, pain, and abuse that happened to me in my life. I began to think that was what life was all about and that I was worth nothing. I had been told so many times by my father that I was worth nothing. My father said I would never amount to anything since I had children at an early age, and at that time, I had not completed high school. I developed lots of issues and had very low self-esteem. At that time in my life I was considered the black sheep in the family. No one really saw the value in me other than my mother. "She always told me that I was a very special child of God and that I could see things most people didn't see.

People tried to make life hard for me because of my gifts. I remember so vividly as if it were yesterday. My mother said, "Almeta, one day God is going to bless and use you in a miraculous way. My mother also said that she may not be here physically to see it, but, she said she would be with me in the spirit cheering me on.

Because of my special gifts, my mother warned me not to speak of the things I am able to see with everyone so that I would not appear to be crazy. She assured me that God would send the right people in my path for me to speak to. She also said that God anointed me with the gift of discernment and interpretation as well as healing in my hands. My mother was my best friend. To God be the glory for the time He allowed her to pour into my spirit. I always shared my visions and dreams with her and interpreted them. I cherished her very much. We would call each other about ten times a day. We would laugh and have a great time sharing our thoughts and experiences. She said I was full of wisdom, just like her own mother. I was named after her mother. When my mother died 1994, I felt as if I was all alone because she always encouraged and loved me unconditionally. There were so many things I was capable of doing, yet could never understand why I never accomplished or completed anything. But, as I looked back over my life, I saw that God had been in control all of the time. I knew He would never leave me nor forsake me, even though at times I thought He did. I know that some of us can relate to this in some form or fashion.

As an adult, by the grace of God, I realized that my subconscious mind believed all the negativity that had been said to me and about me. I believed that I was nothing, would never amount to anything and that I was a disappointment to my family. I asked God to release my mind from that negativity and condition my mind to accept and see that I am a child of The True and Living God. I believe that with God's help, all things are possible.

I also realized, as an adult that father did not intend to hurt me with the words he said to me that I considered mental abuse. He probably experience the same negativity as a child himself. To this day, I truly honor and love my father dearly, not always for his performance, but because of his position in my life. The Word of God teaches us to:

Honor thy father and thy mother: that thy days may be long upon the land which the Lord thy God giveth thee.
Exodus 20:12 KJV

No matter what our experiences, God needs for us to be set apart so that He may do a reconstruction and restoration in our minds and hearts.

But know that the Lord hath set apart him that is godly for himself: the Lord will hear when I call unto him.
Psalm 4:3 KJV

I beseech you therefore, brethren, by the mercies of God, that ye present your bodies a living sacrifice, holy, acceptable unto God, which is your reasonable service. And be not conformed to this world: but be ye transformed by the renewing of your mind, that ye may prove what is that good, and acceptable, and perfect, will of God.
Romans 12:1-2 KJV

I can do all things through Christ who strengthens me.
Philippians 4:13 KJV

No weapon formed against you shall prosper, and every tongue which rises against you in judgment you shall condemn. This is the heritage of the servants of the Lord.
Isaiah 54:17 KJV

For all that is in the world - the lust of the flesh, the lust of the eyes, and the pride of life - is not of the father but is of the world,
1 John 2:16 KJV

I love the Spirit of God that now dwells within me. God's Holy and Divine Spirit motivates me to love others in spite of the way they treat me. My mother always told me to never treat people the way they treat you, rather treat them the way I would want to be treated. My brothers and sisters, we will discover many broken pieces and hurt feelings while in The Sanctuary Within. Be assured that our God has the right formula and is more than equipped to heal and restore all our broken pieces, put them back together again, but this time on a grander scale. So much so that blinded eyes shall be opened, spiritual hearing will be developed, and spiritual cleansing shall take place in our hearts in order for us to be an obedient people.

And when he putted forth his own sheep, He goeth before them, and the sheep follow Him: for they know His voice.
John 10:4 KJV

In order to hear God clearly, we must totally repent of all our sins, even the ones we are not aware of. Being honest with ourselves and giving God all of our problems will set us free. Problems could be that of a broken heart, sickness, diseases, anger, an indiscreet life style, jealousy or pain of any kind. I have learned that when the world becomes too much for us that our God has provided a safe, sacred and secret place for us to go. We can always count on it being there because that place is found in our hearts. We will always be able to connect and trust the Spirit of God within us for the next directions of our lives. This process is very important because we as a chosen people are to become God's Anointed Kings and Queens as we were designed to be.

But you are a chosen generation, a royal priesthood, a holy nation. His own special people, that you may proclaim the praises of him who called you out of darkness into the marvelous light.
1 Peter 2:9 KJV

We are supposed to write the vision and make it plain. How can we make it plain if our minds are so cluttered with the ignorance and arrogance of this world, and not on the things of God?

We must inform the people that serving God is not complicated at all. Those who don't really know God complicate life and its situations. Please remember the attributes that represent our God are all good. Just think, we were originally created in the image of God and after His likeness; but man has since failed and Jesus had to come and show us the way back to a more fruitful and abundant life. Please be aware that upon Finding The Sanctuary Within, people in this world can be very cruel, wicked and unloving.

People don't understand or always care how they make you feel. I truly thank God for His Infinite Wisdom in creating a space we can call The Sanctuary Within. It has truly been a wonderful joy and journey Finding The Sanctuary Within. What makes this place so unique is that the only occupants who can ever enter are

God and us. There we can praise Him, enjoy, love and pray the way we want at any given time. I found so much comfort in the Sanctuary Within. I can now say that I count it all joy.

Have I Not Commanded You? Be Strong And Of Good Courage; Do Not Be Afraid, Nor Be Dismayed, For The Lord Your God Is With You Where Ever You Go.
Joshua 1:9 NKJV

Being in The Sanctuary Within will prove to be a great experience for all of us, we must surrender and let The Spirit of God have His way.

For You formed my inward parts, You covered me in my mother's womb. I will praise You, for I am fearfully and wonderfully made; marvelous are your works. And that my soul knows very well.
Psalms 139:13-14 NKJV

Here is one example for us to take into consideration, while in The Sanctuary Within picture this; here are two glasses of water. The first glass contains all the problems that make our lives miserable and incomplete. These problems will cause you to feel depressed, unwanted, unappreciated, used, disgusted, and unworthy. You can fill the blanks as it applies to your life because only you know your condition. The second glass is that of Pure and Living Water which represents the Spirit of God, which is what our bodies thirst for. The Pure and Living Water of God will cleanse us every time.

Jesus answered and said unto her, whosoever drinketh of this water shall thirst again: but whosoever drinketh of the water that I shall give him shall never thirst; but the water that I shall give him shall be in him a well of water springing up into everlasting life.
John 4:13 KJV

CHAPTER FIVE

OUR SECRET PLACE

The Sanctuary Within is our secret place. In our secret place, God teaches, prepares and anoints us to be more effective in our homes, work place, community and in our church buildings we call the Sanctuary. We will then be able to fellowship, show unconditional love to one another and praise God to the highest level. We must take time for the important things in our lives. We must know that Finding the Sanctuary Within is more valuable than any amount of money or material possessions. I thank God for giving us such a secret place where He is always present. Just know that our God has fashioned us in such a way that no matter where we are in life, this secret and sacred place is within us always. We must also remove ourselves from those who we allow to take us out of the Will of God. We must stop looking outside ourselves to find the love, joy, peace, happiness, kindness, goodness, and faithfulness, which can only come from knowing the Spirit of God within us. The Sanctuary Within is also a place to relax, retreat and restore our spirits.

Are we ready for the Divine change to take place? This change will begin in our minds and flow to our hearts. For our God has the Anointed ability to change our minds about our old ways and habits. We must allow God to help us get our Sanctuary Within in order, so that we will be able to recognize His Divine Holy Spirit within us. God has blessed us to receive spiritual awareness. We are no longer left in darkness because our God has chosen us to be the light of the world.

Then spake Jesus again unto them, saying, I am the light of the world: he that followeth me shall not walk in darkness, but shall have the light of life
John 8:12 KJV

God, I thank You for allowing me to experience Your Divine Unconditional Love, Joy and Peace in the miraculous name of Jesus. My brothers and sisters, imagine how God feels when we acknowledge to others who He is in our lives. When we take the time to share with others our stories and testimonies, it allows others to know how God has kept us in the mist. We have never been perfect, but we strive on a consistent basis to be more Christ like. We have chosen to live a life that's pleasing to God so that we may draw others closer to knowing the real purpose of the life of Jesus Christ.

I became closer to Finding The Sanctuary Within on June 21, 2007. I traveled to San Diego, California for the first time. I had a wonderful time on the plane. As my feet touched new soil, I experienced a new way of living. The purpose of my trip was to speak the Word of God and share my time, love, joy and peace with His people at a Women's Conference. As I listened to God during the conference, I heard God tell me to be still in my spirit and enjoy each day. God said He would reveal more about Finding The Sanctuary Within. He said He would enable me to effectively deposit knowledge of the goodness; power and the love that I had found while Finding The Sanctuary Within, into the lives of others. During the conference, I met many loving and positive people. We toured the waterfront and enjoyed the seafood. After dinner, we continued to walk around on the waterfront and enjoyed the scenery. For the first time, I had an acupuncture treatment to improve balance, it was wonderful. Our next stop was Rancho Santa Fe California. There we visited a ranch with an abundance of lemon trees, strawberry patches and avocado's for as far as the eye could see. Everything was so fresh and delicious. It was the best I had ever tasted. At that time, The Holy Spirit revealed to me that this fresh, delicious and beautiful experience is how the sweetness and love of His Spirit resides in us.

Oh taste and see that the Lord is good. Blessed is the man that trusts in Him.
Psalm 34:8 KJV

The spirit of God also revealed that He was taking me to higher heights, and that it was going to be beyond human comprehension.

But as it is written, eye hath not seen, nor ear heard, neither have entered into the heart of man, the things which God hath prepared for them that love Him.
1 Corinthians 2:9 KJV

My spirit connected so well and I felt so good to be in that place. God truly blessed me, and I thank Him so much for keeping and loving me. My mind began to reflect back in time. At the early age of fifteen, to avoid being disrespectful to my parents I left home. As a fifteen year old I viewed strict up bringing as mental and physical abuse. My siblings and I were whipped and chastised regularly. As an adult I understood that was our parent's way of showing they really loved and cared for us. Well here I was in this big world with first son Alpheus.

By the age of twenty one, I had my other two sons Arthur and Anwar. The streets, older people, and Christian up bringing taught me how to survive in this big cruel world. I had to grow up real fast. I realized long ago that I too, like the Children of Israel, experienced being in the wilderness. I had entered into the wilderness of this wicked world and wandered around for a long time. But God, in His Infinite Wisdom, saw fit to bless me with the opportunity, as a matured adult, to come out of the wilderness a greater and more powerful person having found The Sanctuary Within. The immature Children of Israel choose to do it their own way, rather than obediently doing it God's way, Most of the time we think that we know it all, have all the right answers and want to do it our way. God has already blessed, sanction, ordained and prepared The Sanctuary Within for our spiritual and surgical procedure to take place. We are an imperfect people. Spiritual surgery will prove to be a great benefit for all of us. The Sanctuary Within is where our spiritual surgeon enters. It is so amazing that no anesthesia is ever needed. Just lay back and allow the spiritual surgery to take place in the name of Jesus. Our God is strategically removing anything that stunts our Spiritual Growth. He is getting into all of our cracks and crevasses. He's uprooting all cancer like cells that corrupt the wholesomeness of our bodies and lives. Our God then replaces and refreshes all those diseased areas with His Divine Love, Healing, Peacefulness and Power. Our God is so awesome. Who wouldn't want to serve a God like that? My brothers and sisters, we have moved away from the operating room to the recovery room. There our healing process will take place. During the healing process, remember to thank God for loving us enough to heal and mature us with a new level of understanding as to who He is in our lives. Now we can become the bright illuminators for this world. We are a blessed people who are able to freely commune with God at any time of day, about anything. The line will never be busy, never a bad connection, or concern about any gossip being spread. Our God has ordained it so that we can openly share all our problems, our fears, our insecurities, desires and our needs with Him. What a magnificent God we serve. The challenge is, learning to be quiet, have patience and wait, so that we may hear our God when He answers us. Please know that when our God answers, it may not always be what we want to hear.

There are three ways God will answer us:

1. He may say yes.
2. He may say no.
3. He may be silent or just say be still, now is not the appointed time.

It is very important to know that anything concerning our God is True, Sacred, has a Divine Time, a Divine Order, and Divine Purpose so that it will accomplish His Perfect Divine Plan and Will. Please try not to step out of the Will of God because the consequences are too high.

To everything there is a season, and a time to every purpose under the heaven;
Ecclesiastes 3:1 KJV

God is a Spirit: and they that worship him must worship him in spirit and in truth.
John 4:24 KJV

Now the LORD *is that Spirit: and where the Spirit of the* LORD *is, there is liberty.*
2 Corinthians 3:17 KJV

In some of my past relationships and situations, I kept many ungodly secrets. When my spiritual surgery took place, I became wiser and more mature. I understood that anything godly did not have to be kept secret. In the Sanctuary Within, we may have a secret, sacred friendship and relationship with our God because it is a personal thing. He relates to everyone according to their personal needs in the healing name of Jesus. We can be open and reveal all of the personal feelings we have in our hearts. In addition, we discover that our Most High, Holy and Divine God also bless us to never feel inadequate, or rejected. Moreover the truth is, we have the liberty of finding out that we really are in Him and He is in us. In order to reach, receive and stay connected to our God we must put ourselves in a Holy State of Consciousness to be able to relate to the Spirit of God within us.

While in The Sanctuary Within, we must continue to allow God to nurture our faith, trust and belief system, for He is preparing us to be a people of Divine Purpose in The Holy Name of Jesus Christ.

CHAPTER SIX

EXPLORING THE SANCTUARY WITHIN

As we continue to explore The Sanctuary Within, we can all say that at some point in our lives, we were in a backslidden state. Know that our God is married to the backslider. God will never divorce us because He loves us, no matter what we do or have done. He is always ready to receive and deliver us from our wicked ways. God allows us to make the necessary U-turn to come back to him. God is waiting to prepare us for our personal assignments in this earthly realm. Know that our God is here for us at all times. As we explore the Sanctuary Within, we become enlightened as to who we are and recognize our self-worth as well as see ourselves in a different light. We are privileged to be able to ask our God to take away our carnal minds and renew in us a spiritual mindset that reflects the mind of Christ. We must also ask God to change our natural hearing to a spiritual hearing that we only hear the things He chooses for us to hear.

God please remove the blinders from our natural eyes and open our spiritual eyes so that we may see the things you have designed for our eyes to see. God we ask that you take away this old heart of ours and give us a pure and sincere heart that is fitting for Your service. God we pray that You move our feet from places they should not go. Please order our steps in Your Perfect Divine Way that we may walk where You need and have ordained us to walk. God, please bless our old dirty hands and anoint them to only touch what you have designed them to touch. God, please wash and change our worldly mouths from filthy to spiritual, suited to glorify and edify You when we speak. God, I pray and ask You to continue to cover our minds with the blood of Jesus. Use us as You see fit for the benefit of Your Kingdom here on earth.

CHAPTER SEVEN

BEING IN THE SANCTUARY WITHIN

Being in The Sanctuary not only means it is a place to be quiet, but also a place to be still and rest in our spirits as well. Resting can also include meditating, deep breathing and being open so God can freely pour into our spirit. Being in The Sanctuary Within is a time in our lives where we are secluded from all the cares of this world, where our time is totally devoted to our God in prayer and being obedient to His Perfect Divine Will. Nothing should ever get in the way of us taking care of ourselves.

Being in The Sanctuary Within reminded me that I had been saved as a young person who had strayed away. I was able to reflect back when I enjoyed being in the world. I grew up in a good Christian home, but as a young person, I enjoyed being in the world. I attended Bible Way Holiness Church in Washington, DC under the leadership of Bishop Smallwood E. Williams. I was taught and studied the Word of God all the time. I was in church all day long on Sundays and at least three times during the week. At that time, I hated that church and the people in it. As a child I saw and experienced so many ungodly things and I was really hurt by church people. As a result, I left the church and vowed never to return.

I ventured out into the wilderness to experience what the church or my parents never allowed us to do. I thought I was stepping in high cotton as the older folks would say. There where so many city lights, lots of action, parties, singing, dancing, joking and all kinds of food, movies and music. Dancing was my favorite thing to do. I could dance very well and it was really fun learning all of the new steps. I tried several things to get high such as acid, pcp, angel dust, heroin and cocaine, following the crowd in order to fit in. All of which could have destroyed my mind. I wasn't addicted to any of it. I thank God for keeping and protecting me in my foolish ways. So many people are hurting in this world and in our churches today for some of the same reasons.

I am able to recognize the pain in others, maybe you can relate in some form or fashion. If you've ever experienced being there than you can fill in the blanks as it relates to you. When I was younger, I knew that some of the things adults did and said was wrong. Adults would always say, "do as I say not as I do." As children we mimic what we see and hear. I thought I knew everything until one day as an adult; I really met Jesus on a whole new level. Today, I have a spiritual party that goes on and on. The music never stops and the lights are always on because we are the light of the world. Now that I am no longer on the world's time clock, there is a difference in me. I have also changed dance partners, I no longer dance to the tune of the world, rather I now dance for our God in the Spirit of Holiness. What a marvelous change that has come over me. It feels even better being on the Lords side. If He did it for a wretch like me, He will surely do it for you. The Holy Spirit informed me that all of our lives are at stake. Being in The Sanctuary Within will enlighten and benefit us greatly. In The Sanctuary Within, all those dark places in our lives are exposed and it allows us to focus and get balance so that the true light of our God can shine through us on a daily basis. That is why it's so easy for me to recognize and have a heart for those who are hurting and have fallen by the wayside.

I want you to know that our God kept and healed me through the process and will do the same for all of us. So many people are hurting because of a lack of real unconditional love, being rejected, fearful, being disregarded and a lack of love for one's self. These kinds of people often unknowingly hurt others. This is why it so important for this generational curse to be broken. We need to thank God for allowing His Son Jesus to come and bridge the gap for all mankind. We now have easy access to our God because of the obedience of our Lord and Savior Jesus Christ. There is no reason for any of us to be blind about anything. Jesus has already paid the price and made the way possible for us.

He was wounded for our transgressions; he was bruised for our iniquities: the chastisement of our peace was upon Him; and with His stripes we are healed.
Isaiah 53:5 KJV

When the light of God is in us we can't just live any old kind of way. God has saved and blessed us and it is imperative that we live a transparent life for God so that we may be a true blessing and an asset to others.

But if we walk in the light, as he is in the light, we have fellowship one with another, and the blood of Jesus Christ His Son cleanseth us from all sin
1John 1:7 KJV

Spirit of the living God please fill and bless this place called The Sanctuary Within.

I press toward the mark for the prize of the high calling of God in Christ Jesus.
Philippians 3:14 KJV

There is one thing in this world that we can do far greater than anyone else, and that is being our own unique self and being true to ourselves. Another great benefit of spending quality time in The Sanctuary Within is that it makes us a stronger people who become carbon copies of authenticity. Let's ask ourselves a very important question. Are we as a body of baptized believers in the Lord Jesus Christ, totally being faithful to our calling? If we are not, it will be impossible for us to advance in the service of our God until we change our attitudes. For it is truly a blessing to be in the Perfect Will of God. Being in the Sanctuary Within also allows each one of us to have our own personal relationship with God. He then rewards us with His Perfect Divine Revelatory Knowledge. It is also imperative for us to receive all of what our God needs to pour into our spirits so that we might be prepared for the next dimension in our lives.

Our God has set an awesome task before us. Our task is to live a life that helps to bring others out of the pits of their lives, to a life that is pleasing for His service in the Name of Jesus. We are all chosen vessels of the True and Living God. Please remember that what we do and say has an effect on others. We must be in line and in tune with the Will of God so that we may pour into the lives of others the correct way. For those who do not wish to receive the blessings, ways and teaching of our Lord and Savior Jesus Christ, just leave them alone and put them into the hands of God. My brothers and sisters, there is a dying world out there and there are so many people who are in search of the truth and a better way of living. Let us plant good seeds into the heart of mankind. We do not have to wait around to see the results, because some seeds need more nurturing than others. God, in His appointed time, will make sure those seeds takes root and grow in the awesome Name of Jesus. The word of God says:

And whosoever shall not receive you, nor hear your words, when ye depart out of that house or city, shake off the dust of your feet.
Matthew 10:14 KJV

As I reflect over my life as a young person, I was truly blessed and loved tremendously by kind, caring and elderly people who richly poured into my life an enormous amount of valuable information. Even though I strayed, I never forgot the positive seeds and words of wisdom that were planted into my life. They would tell me that I had been here before and that I was an old soul. My goal is to give back to others in that same manner. I am here by the Grace of God. Today I can truly say, with true conviction and not take it for granted, that I am here by the Grace of God. God's Divine Grace and Unmerited Favor are truly upon my life, so it shall be for everyone who trusts him. Many of my associates along the way are suffering with some sort of illness, incarcerated or dead. I say associates because I use the word friend very lightly.

I know that God has kept me here in my right mind and in good health for such a time as this. So it is with all of us that we might be a greater blessing to His people. Let's get a grip and stop disappointing God with all of our foolishness. Let us move forward in this beautiful life with the mind and heart that has been transformed to the newness of Christ, for we are truly the representation of our God in an awesome way.

CHAPTER EIGHT

HEALING IN THE SANCTUARY WITHIN

If my people, which are called by my name, shall humble themselves, and pray, and seek my face, and turn from their wicked ways; then will I hear from heaven, and will forgive their sin, and will heal their land.
2 Chronicles 7:14 KJV

When we go out into the world as Disciples of Christ, we will see many people are walking around looking good but they are in a serious state of pain on the inside. This is why they are not able to get along with others. When you look at a person from the outside they really look good and appear to be alright, but on the inside they are broken and torn apart. There is an old saying "Never judge a book by its cover." People always told me that I always looked so nice, that I had a pleasant smile on my face all of the time and that I always had something kind to say to others. I give my Mother the honor for that because of the way she taught me. My mother always told me never let people in your business or see the sadness on your face, but always greet them as if I were greeting Jesus. To this day, I still follow her teachings. I have always been wise and willing to assist others with their problems but fell short when it came to my own problems. I was a grown woman with a little child locked up on the inside with so many problems. Now that I know better I can do better, ignorance can no longer be used as an excuse for any of us. Here is a few questions to ponder in our minds:

1. *Who Am I in The kingdom Of God?*
2. *Why Am I Here?*
3. *What Am I Suppose To Do?*
4. *Where Am I In Terms Of My Relationship With God?*
5. *Whose Am I God Or The Devil?*
6. *And What Kind of Seed do I truly represent?*

God is the creator of the universe. He is also the creator of us all. We all need to allow His Will to be done in our lives. The enemy is coming after us by any means necessary. His goal has always been to try to trick us. Please be advised, the evil spirit is very slick, cunning, and crafty and has many tactics to fool us. We must remain focused, absorb God's Word in our hearts and not allow the evil one to creep into our lives. We must stay in tune with whose and whom we are and not lose ourselves in other people. That is why Finding The Sanctuary Within has proven to be very essential for our well-being.

With my whole heart have I sought thee: o let me not wander from thy commandments. Thy word have I hid in mine heart, which I might not sin against thee.
Psalms 119:10-11 KJV

And now these three remain: faith, hope and love. But the greatest of these is love.
I Corinthians 13:13 KJV

My brothers and sisters, unconditional love is the key. We must stay focus so that fear and hate will not kill our spirit, family, dreams, homes, ministries and communities. Our health is also controlled by the spirit we house within.

THE QUESTION IS: Are we displaying a good spirit or a bad spirit? This is why it's so important to be aware of our surrounding. Spirits do not jump into walls or things, rather they jump into us and we begin to act strangely.

God is concern with what we house on the inside which should be a right heart and spirit. I thank God for blessing me with The Right Spirit, His Unconditional Love, Divine Power, and a Forgiving Heart. This blessing is available to all of us.

Then Peter opened his mouth, and said, of a truth I perceive that God is no respecter of persons;
Acts 10:34 KJV

I thank God for the ministry of healing that He has placed in my heart and hands. I also thank God for allowing me to be one of His anointed and appointed prayer warriors and intercessors. God I thank you so much for gifting me to love the foolishness out of others.

MY PRAYER IS: God I honor and worship you, I praise You and love you with my whole heart. God I ask that You fill all the voids in our lives with Your Divine Spirit. God we thank you in advance for defining every detail in all our lives. God I ask that you make known, bless and nurture each gift in every one of us in the Providing Name of Jesus. Amen!

God I thank you for Bishop Glen Alonzo Staples who preached and taught all of those life changing sermons that confirmed that I was in the right place and moving in the right direction. God never promised us that our process would be easy. When He anoints and appoints us, He gives us the necessary tools and strengths to withstand any of the fiery darts that are designed to block us from our assignments. Amen.

For it is written as I live, says the Lord, every knee shall bow to me, and every tongue shall confess to God.
Romans 14:11 KJV

And if the Spirit of him who raised Jesus from the dead is living in you, he who raised Christ from the dead will also give life to your mortal bodies because of his Spirit who lives in you.
Romans 8:11 NIV

GOD IS THE DIVINE HEALER OF OUR LIVES

Beloved, I wish above all things that thou mayest prosper and be in health, even as thy soul prospereth.
3 John 2 KJV

He that spared not His own Son, but delivered Him up for us all, how shall he not with him also freely give us all things?
Romans 8:32 KJV

CHAPTER NINE

PASTORS AND LEADERS

Finding The Sanctuary Within is an absolute must for pastors and leaders because this world is not looking too good these days. We seem to be in a very deep sleep. So much is going on and nobody seems to be addressing the real problems. The Bible has been left here as our blueprint for life, and we cannot pick and choose what we are going to teach and talk about. This society is in a tremendous storm and we are going straight to hell if we don't wake up, surrender our will unto God and be obedient to His word. Even in our churches so many people are hurting and perishing. Some have been there for a while and others are new comers. They come into the house of God looking for spiritual help to live a better life. But what do they find there; the church is asleep as well. We are allowing all sorts of ungodly things to take place in the house of God. We are really disappointing God. God directs the people to the church of which I say is a hospital for sick people to get well. None of us are exempt from some sort of healing and restoration. We all have some type of illness. These illnesses could be in the form of adultery, fornication, stealing, homosexuality, an unforgiving spirit and no real love for one another. The list can go on and on. This only brings a DIS-EASE to the Body of Christ. In the Body of Christ there is supposed to be healing, deliverance and restoration for those who are captured and need to be set free. And we, who are the matured in Christ, must have patience and love God's people unconditionally. Most of all, God's unconditional love should be our highest aim.

When I say to a wicked person, "You will surely die," and you do not warn them or speak out to dissuade them from their evil ways in order to save their life, that wicked person will die for their sin, and I will hold you accountable for their blood.
Ezekiel 3:18 NIV

And I will give you shepherds according to My heart, who will feed you with knowledge and understanding.
Jeremiah 3:15 NKJV

SHEPHERDS AND GOD'S SHEEP

The word of the Lord came to me: Son of man, prophesy against the shepherds of Israel. Prophesy and say to them, this is what the sovereign Lord says: "Woe to the shepherds of Israel who only take care of themselves! Should not shepherds take care of the flock? You eat the curds, clothe yourselves with the wool and slaughter the choice animals. But you do not take care of the flock. You have not strengthened the weak or healed the sick or bound up the injured. You have not brought back the strays or searched for the lost. You have ruled them harshly and brutally. They were scattered because there was no shepherd, and when they were scattered they became food for all the wild animals. My sheep wandered over all the mountains and on every high hill. They were scattered over the whole earth and no one searched or looked for them. Therefore, you shepherds, hear the word of the Lord, "As surely as I live," declares the sovereign Lord, because my flock lacks a shepherd and so has been plundered, and has become food for all the wild animals, and because my shepherds did not search for my flock but cared for themselves rather than for my flock, therefore, oh shepherds, hear the word of the Lord. This is what the sovereign Lord says, I am against the shepherds and will hold them accountable for my flock. I will remove them from tending the flock so that the shepherds can no longer feed themselves. I will rescue my flock from their mouths and it will no longer be food for them.

For this is what the sovereign Lord says, "I myself will search for My sheep and look after them. As a shepherd looks after his scattered flock when he is with them, so will I look after my sheep? I will rescue them from all the places where they were scattered on a day of clouds and darkness. I will bring them out from the nations and gather them from the countries, and I will bring them into their own land. I will pasture them on the mountains of Israel, in the ravines and in all the settlements in the land. I will tend them in a good pasture and the mountain heights of Israel will be their grazing land. There they will lie down in good grazing land, and there they will feed in a rich pasture on the mountains of Israel. I, Myself, will tend my sheep and have them lie down declares the sovereign Lord. I will search for the lost and bring back the strays. I will bind up the injured and strengthen the weak, but the sleek and the strong I will destroy. I will shepherd the flock with justice. As for you, my flock, this is what the sovereign Lord says, I will judge between one sheep and another, and between rams and goats. Is it not enough for you to feed on the good pasture? Must you also trample the rest of your pasture with your feet? Is it not enough for you to drink clear water? Must you also muddy the rest with your feet? Must My flock feed on what you have trampled and drink what you have muddied with your feet?" Therefore, this is what the sovereign Lord says to them. See, I, Myself, will judge between the fat sheep and the lean sheep. Because you shove with flank and shoulder, butting all the weak sheep with your horns until you have driven them away, I will save my flock and they will no longer be plundered. I will judge between one sheep and another. I will place over them one shepherd, My servant David, and he will tend them. He will tend them and be their shepherd. I, the Lord, will be their God and My servant David will be prince among them. I, the Lord, have spoken. I will make a covenant of peace with them and rid the land of wild beasts so that they may live in the desert and sleep in the forests in safety. I will bless them and the places surrounding my hill. I will send down showers in season. There will be showers of blessings. The trees of the field will yield their fruit and the ground will yield its crops. The people will be secure in their land. They will know that I am the Lord

when I break the bars of their yoke and rescue them from the hands of those who enslaved them. They will no longer be plundered by the nations, nor will wild animals devour them. They will live in safety and no one will make them afraid. I will provide for them a land renowned for its crops, and they will no longer be victims of famine in the land or bear the scorn of the nations. Then they will know that I, the Lord their God, am with them and that they, the house of Israel, are my people declares the sovereign Lord. You, my sheep, the sheep of my pasture, are people and I am your God" declares the sovereign Lord.
Ezekiel 34 NIV

My brothers and sisters, we must get it right if we profess to know and love Jesus Christ. We, as leaders, are not suppose to cause people to stumble. We are supposed to pick them up and lead them in the right direction. We need to then allow God to mold and shape us in His Own Perfect Divine Way for His Divine Purpose. We are supposed to be living examples for others. We are all teachers and leaders in some form or fashion, whether we're teaching them to do what's right or wrong, it's being taught one way or the other. So let's ask ourselves, "What kind of teacher am I? We do not want to be one of those who are just playing church for their own selfish reasons."

My brethren, let not many of you become teachers, knowing that we shall receive a stricter judgment.
James 3:1 NKJV

Beloved, do not believe every spirit, but test the spirits, whether they are of God because many false prophets have gone out into the world.
1 John 4:1 NKJV

LEADERS, we cannot keep allowing the devil or the evil spirit to have all this power and control in our churches. I've always wondered why is there so much turmoil, division and schism going on in the Body of Christ, and why is it that everyone could not fellowship together? I knew of several churches in a three block radius, and none of them would even fellowship with one another. This is why the community at large is in such disarray, and so many people have fallen by the wayside. The lack of love we have for one another has really caused an imbalance to the Body of Christ, as well as the community. We claim to love God, whom we cannot see, and don't display the same kind of love for our brothers and sisters who we do see on a regular basis. There is something truly wrong with this picture. If we are supposed to be a representation of who God is, we must show unconditional love to everyone. God is no respecter of persons; we must remember who we are, a representative of the True and Living God. I love everyone in the Matchless Majestic and Mighty Name of Jesus Christ. And because I do, I am praying for the deliverance of such foolishness and immaturity to stop. And for all pastor's and leaders who hold any kind of title, I pray that God's daily transformation take place in all lives concerned. Please know that our God has given us an awesome assignment of leading and directing His people to the realization of who He is in their lives. True humbleness on our behalf is essential so that we may receive God's Divine Direction for our lives, as well as others. Please be informed that the carnal side of us can really make us think we are right. That evil spirit really has the capability of blinding us in that area. The Word of God is so powerful, and it says to serve me in Spirit and Truth. God wants us to find the sheep and feed them.

We should not manipulate or pimp them in any fashion. Just know that in our God's appointed time, He shall deal with those wicked leaders who lead His sheep astray and hurts them in any way.

He said to him the third time, "Simon, son of Jonah, do you love me?" Peter was grieved because He said to him the third time, "Do you love Me? And he said to Him, "Lord, you know all things; You know that I love You." Jesus said to him, Feed my sheep."
John 21:17 NKJV

WHAT KIND OF LEADER'S ARE WE?

Leaders that have been divinely chosen by God will nurture and develop the Body of Christ into a strong cohesive family. God is looking for leaders with an authentic heart, and that of a humble spirit for His service. I truly thank God for my Bishop, Glen Alonzo Staples, who is humbled, saved, anointed and has the heart of God. He studies and teaches the Body of Christ from the Word of God. Under Bishop Staples' watch many have been saved, healed, delivered and set free. Bishop Staples also teaches and stresses to the people of God the importance of education, so that they may live and lead more productive lives. My brothers and sisters, this generation, now and the generations to come, need more leaders who have the heart of God that will really love, nurture, feed and lead His people the correct way in the healing, loving and peaceful Name of Jesus.

I, Jesus, have sent My angel to testify to you these things in the churches. I am the Root and the Offspring of David, the Bright and Morning Star." And the Spirit and the bride say, "Come." And let him

who hear say, "Come." And let him who thirsts, "Come." Whosoever desires, let him take the water of life freely. For I testify to everyone who hears the words of the prophecy of this book: "If anyone adds to these things, God will add to him the plagues that are written in this book."
Revelations 22:16-18 NKJV

I PRAY THAT THE ANOINTED POWER OF GOD REST UPON US ALL

Most assuredly, I say to you, "He who believes in Me, the works that I do he will do also; and greater works than these he will do because I go to My Father."
John 14:12 NKJV

GOD HAS ALSO SUPPLIED US WITH EVERYTHING WE NEED

But seek first the kingdom of God and His righteousness, and all these things shall be added unto you".
Matthew 6:33 NKJV

Brethren, if anyone among you wanders from the truth, and someone turns him back, let him know that he who turns a sinner from the error of his way will save a soul from death and cover a multitude of sins.
James 5:19-20 NKJV

CHAPTER TEN

EMERGING FROM THE SANCTUARY WITHIN

RADIATE THE BRILLIANCE OF GOD.

When we emerge from Finding The Sanctuary Within, we shall really know who we are in Christ; we shall have the Divine ability to worship God in Spirit and in Truth. In addition, we must continue to read, listen, and study the Word of God so that it may feed our spirit on a daily basis. When we line up with the Will of God, it increases our love, faith, wisdom, knowledge and understanding. Once we emerge from The Sanctuary Within, people will know that we have been in the Divine Presence of The Holy Spirit. It will be just like when Moses had that mountain top experience with God when the Ten Commandments were being written. Moses neither looked nor was he ever the same. The brilliance of our God was upon him, as it shall be with us. We too will radiate the brilliance of God. It really benefits us to follow the leading of God for every area and detail of our lives.

CHOICES AND DECISIONS

I must keep emphasizing that it's very easy to make the wrong choices and decisions. That's why it takes the Word of God to make the difference in us. We must always put God first in our lives so that He can show us the way to make the right choices and decisions. Remember that following God also brings a balance to and in our lives as well. We must avail ourselves to be used by God at all times even if it hurts. Just know that we all have something in us that would benefit this world. God has planted and cultivated some magnificent seeds in all of us. My brothers and sisters, its harvest time, so let's get it right because time is winding up. We must ask ourselves, "What kind of seeds are we planting in the heart of God's people. Are they seeds of good or seeds of evil?" Now that we have entered, explored and enjoyed being in The Sanctuary Within, it is safe to come out now. We have been blessed with the Holy Ghost Power, and a Higher Level of Anointing has been placed upon our lives. We should not take that lightly because the Divine Spirit of God reigns in us. Imagine this: We are now ready to be great examples for others. We are now prepared to meet and grace the people of God and be true witnesses to them. The Red Sea has been parted in our lives. God is waiting for us to cross over to the other side. What are we waiting for?

The thief does not except to steal, and to kill, and to destroy. I have come that they may have life and that they may have it more abundantly.
John 10:10 NKJV

Finding The Sanctuary Within has now prepared and enhanced the church in us. We are the church and we bring our church into the building/sanctuary to fellowship, to worship, to love one another, to praise and to serve God in spirit and truth. How can we be effective without Finding The Sanctuary Within? God calls His special people to do a great work for Him. I find that when we make the Word of God a priority in our daily lives, it becomes a lot easier to be obedient. We should know now that anything God allows in our life must first be sifted through Him. We must remain steadfast and faithful as we move along life's journey. We should continue to put God first in our lives. I'm sure there will be many tests in the pursuit to being happy. Please stay focused and anchored in God, knowing He will withhold no good thing from us. God is always with us. He will always reveal to us everything we need to know about situations or people. Everything we do must be done in the right Spirit, through the Spirit, by the Spirit and for the Spirit of God. We must also wait on God to send the right people to be in our lives. Just know that they may neither look nor talk like we think they should. We often look for people to be a certain kind of way. And because we don't wait on the leading of God, we often choose people that will hurt or abuse us. That is not who or what God has for our lives. The ones God has chosen and ordained shall cherish, love, support and adore us.

Finally, brethren, whatever things are true, whatever things are noble, whatever things are just, whatever things are pure, whatever things are lovely, whatever things are of good report, if there is any virtue and if there is anything praiseworthy - meditate on these things.
Philippians 4:8 NKJV

I will praise You for I am fearfully and wonderfully made; marvelous are Your works, and that my soul knows very well.
Psalm 139:14 NKJV

I myself am convinced, my brothers and sisters, that you yourselves are full of goodness, filled with knowledge, and competent to instruct one another. Yet I have written you quite boldly on some points to remind you of them again, because of the grace God gave me to be a minister of Christ Jesus to the Gentiles. He gave me the priestly duty of proclaiming the gospel of God so that the Gentiles might become an offering acceptable to God, sanctified by the Holy Spirit.
Romans 15:14-16 NIV

CHAPTER ELEVEN

A NEW PERSON IN CHRIST

There has now been a great spiritual change in all of our lives. The change first took place in our minds and then it flowed down into our hearts. God's Anointed Power has changed our minds about our old ways and habits. Finding, being, exploring and coming out of The Sanctuary Within has been an awesome blessing to our lives. We are now new creative people in Christ. My brothers and sisters just know that God never intended for His Word to be complicated. So as we continue to read, listen and study His word, we must ask Him for clarity, understanding and the interpretation. Remember that God gave us our joy and peace back, so don't allow the enemy anything or anyone to steal or disturb us in any way. Remember the enemy works through people to kill, destroy and conquer us. Just know that he's only working with limited power. The only power the enemy has in our lives is what we allow him to have. God has all power and because we are an extension of God, we too have the power to rebuke anything that is not like Him. Let us be happy with what God has blessed our lives with. And know that when we love, trust and believe God life becomes a little more tolerant and pleasant for us. I know now that part of my mission is to win souls for Christ, to minister and encourage pastors and leaders on their continuous walk for Christ. God holds the key to all of our lives. So don't worry. Your quest might be a little different from mine, but we all have one. So take the time to ask God to reveal what our purpose is and permit Him to nurture it in the Name of Jesus. We are all a vision of God and the apple of His eyes, and with the leading of The Holy Spirit we shall all make it plain to others in the name of Jesus. We are to touch the lives of all of God's people no matter what state they are in. And let it be known that we, as baptized believers in the Body of Christ, are supposed to teach others that Christ died for all of our sins. There are no big I's or little U's, no little or big sins; sin is sin and it is our duty as believers to show love and kindness towards all people.

For all have sinned and fall short of the glory of God.
Romans 3:23 NIV

We have everything in God. He tells us that we are His children and that we don't have to worry or want for anything. Whatever we are asking God for, we have the power to speak it into existence as long as it is according to our God's Divine Will, Time, Purpose and Destiny for our lives. Remember that our God is more than able to provide us with everything we need. What I am saying is we really do not need it if God has not ordained it. It may be anything from a thought, word, deed, a relationship, or a since of purpose we are supposed to follow.

Please fill in the blanks as it applies to you. I pray that as the days go on that we continue to allow the Sweet Spirit of God to fill any voids we may have in our lives with His Divine Love and Power.

PRAYER

Father God, in the blessed name of Jesus, I pray that we draw closer to you and one another in the Sweet Spirit of Love. Father God, I ask that you please continue to bless, deliver, strengthen and anoint us in The Healing Name of Your Son, Our Savior Jesus Christ. My brothers and sisters, doesn't it feel good now that we have opened our hearts to embrace the divine and sweet Spirit of God within us? Thank you so much for taking this journey with me on "Finding The Sanctuary Within". Just know that we have been saturated with our God's Divine Anointing and Miraculous Power. Also, I pray that we continue to let God help us keep our sanctuaries in divine order. Please remember that The Sanctuary Within is the dwelling place for the Holy Spirit. We give thanks to our God for making a way for us to have such a sacred place called The Sanctuary Within. Through all we had to endure, remember that the pain was never to defeat us, it is to promote us to a higher level of anointing. By Finding The Sanctuary Within our greatest benefit is that our God has enlightened us on how to forgive, love others, and to appreciate the intimate fellowship of love and respect we have with Him. Amen.

O God, You are my God; early will I seek You; my soul thirsts for You; my flesh longs for You in a dry and thirsty land where there is no water. So I have looked for You in the sanctuary to see Your power and Your glory. Because Your loving kindness is better than life, My lips shall praise You. Thus I will bless You while I live; I will lift up my hands in Your name.
Psalm 63:1-4 NKJV

I will bless the Lord at all times; His praise shall continually be in my mouth. My soul shall make its boast in the Lord; the humble shall hear of it and be glad. Oh, magnify the Lord with me and let us exalt His name together. I sought the Lord. He heard me and delivered me from all my fears. They looked to Him and were radiant, and their faces were not ashamed. This poor man cried out and the Lord heard him, and saved him out of all his troubles. The angel of the Lord encamps all around those who fear Him, and delivers them. Oh, taste and see that the Lord is good; blessed is the man who trusts in Him! Oh, fear the Lord, you His saints! There is no want to those who fear Him. The young lack and

suffer hunger; but those who seek the Lord shall not lack any good thing. Come, you children, listen to Me; I will teach you the fear of the Lord. Who is the man who desires life, and loves many days, that he may see good? Keep your tongue from evil, and your lips from speaking deceit. Depart from evil and do good; seek peace and pursue it. The eyes of the Lord are on the righteous, and His ears are open to their cry. The face of the Lord is against those who do evil to cutoff the remembrance of them from the earth. The righteous cry out and the Lord hears, and delivers them out of all their troubles. The Lord is near to those who have a broken heart, and saves such as have a contrite spirit. Many are the afflictions of the righteous, but the Lord delivers him out of them all. He guards all his bones; not one of them is broken. Evil shall slay the wicked, and those who hate the righteous shall be condemned. The Lord redeems the soul of His servants, and none of those who trust in Him shall be condemned.
Psalm 34:1-22 NKJV

For the LORD God is a sun and shield; the LORD will give grace and glory; no good thing will He withhold from those who walk uprightly.
Psalm 84:11 NKJV

We should now feel God's Powerful Energy continuously moving in our spirits? That energy gives us the power to have a renewed mind and heart, which enables us to have a much more matured soul, making us new creative people in Christ. It is our responsibility to teach others about salvation. Salvation is free to all who believe in Jesus Christ, and it shall supply them with a new perspective on life. Never put total trust in any human because they have limited power and they will disappoint us every time. God has all power and He blesses us with His Divine Power and Christian qualities.

But He said to me, "My grace is sufficient for you, for my power is made perfect in weakness." Therefore, I will boast all the more gladly about my weaknesses, so that Christ's power may rest on me.
2 Corinthians 12:9 NIV

OUR GOD'S DIVINE POWER HAS GIVEN US EVERYTHING WE NEED FOR LIFE

And because of that He has given us His very great and precious promises, so that through that we may participate in His Divine Nature and escape the corruption in the world caused by evil desires.

His divine power has given us everything we need for a godly life through our knowledge of him who called us by his own glory and goodness. Through these he has given us his very great and precious promises, so that through them you may participate in the divine nature, having escaped the corruption in the world caused by evil desires.

For this very reason, make every effort to add to your faith goodness; and to goodness, knowledge; and to knowledge, self-control; and to self-control, perseverance; and to perseverance, godliness; and to godliness, mutual affection; and to mutual affection, love. For if you possess these qualities in increasing measure, they will keep you from being ineffective and unproductive in your knowledge of our Lord Jesus Christ. But whoever does not have them is nearsighted and blind, forgetting that they have been cleansed from their past sins.

Therefore, my brothers and sisters,] make every effort to confirm your calling and election. For if you do these things, you will never stumble and you will receive a rich welcome into the eternal kingdom of our Lord and Savior Jesus Christ.
2 Peter 1:3-18 NIV

PROPHECY OF SCRIPTURE

So I will always remind you of these things, even though you know them and are firmly established in the truth you now have. I think it is right to refresh your memory as long as I live in the tent of this body, because I know that I will soon put it aside, as our Lord Jesus Christ has made clear to me. And I will make every effort to see that after my departure you will always be able to remember these things.

For we did not follow cleverly devised stories when we told you about the coming of our Lord Jesus Christ in power, but we were eyewitnesses of His majesty. He received honor and glory from God the Father when the voice came to him from the Majestic Glory, saying, "This is my Son, whom I love; with him I am well pleased. We ourselves heard this voice that came from heaven when we were with Him on the sacred mountain.

2 Peter 1:3-8 NIV

CHAPTER TWELVE

RECEIVING THE ANOINTING OF THE HOLY SPIRIT

When we have a divine relationship with our God, He blesses and anoints us with the Power of The Holy Spirit so that we are able to reach others. Here are some pearls of wisdom for a transformed life.

We must trust God at all times and receive His Divine Anointing for our life. God's favor outweighs anything. Let no one steal our joy or anything that God has given us.

You shall anoint them, as you anointed their father, that they may minister to Me as priests; for their anointing shall surely be an everlasting priesthood throughout their generations.
Exodus 40:15 NKJV

You shall not go out from the door of the tabernacle of meeting, lest you die; for the anointing oil of the Lord is upon you. And they did according to the word of Moses.
Leviticus 10:7 NKJV

He who is the high priest among his brethren, on whose head the anointing oil was poured, and who is consecrated to the garments, shall not uncover his head nor tear his clothes. Nor shall he go out of the sanctuary, nor profane the sanctuary of his God; for the consecration of the anointing oil of his God is upon him: I am the Lord.
Leviticus 21:10, 12 NKJV

THE HOLY SPIRIT IS ETERNAL

*Dear children, this is the last hour; and as you have heard that the antichrist is coming, even now many antichrists have come. This is how we know it is the last hour. They went out from us, but they did not really belong to us. For if they had belonged to us, they would have remained with us; but their going showed that none of them belonged to us. But you have an anointing from the Holy One, and all of you know the truth. I do not write to you because you do not know the truth, but because you do know it and because no lie comes from the truth. Who is the liar? It is **whoever** denies that Jesus is the Christ. Such a person is the antichrist – **denying** the Father and the Son. No one who denies the Son has the Father; whoever acknowledges the Son has the Father also. **As for you, see** that what you have heard from the beginning remains in you. If it does, you also will remain in the Son and in the Father. And this is what He promised us – eternal life. I am writing these things to you about those who are trying to lead you astray. As for you, the anointing you received from Him remains in you, and you do not need anyone to teach you. But as His anointing teaches you about all things and as that anointing is real, not counterfeit – just as it has taught you, remain in Him.*
1 John 2:18-27 NIV

THE HOLY SPIRIT IS OMNIPRESENT

How much more shall the blood of Christ, who the eternal Spirit offered Himself without spot to God, cleanse your conscience from dead works to serve the living God?
Hebrews 9:14 NKJV

THE HOLY SPIRIT IS OMNISCIENT

Where can I go from your Spirit? Where can I flee from your presence? If I go up to the heavens, you are there; if I make my bed in the depths, you are there. If I rise on the wings of the dawn, if I settle on the far side of the sea, even there your hand will guide me; your right hand will hold me fast. If I say, "Surely the darkness will hide me and the light becomes night around me," even the darkness will not be dark to you; the night will shine like the day, for darkness is as light to you. For you created my inmost being; you knit me together in my mother's womb.
Psalm 139:7-13 NIV -

THE HOLY SPIRIT IS OMNIPOTENT

*But God has revealed **them** to us **through** His Spirit. **For the** Spirit searches all things, yes, and the deep things of God.*
1 Corinthians 2:10 NKJV

May the God of hope fill you with all joy and peace as you trust in Him, so that you may overflow with hope by the power of the Holy Spirit.
Romans 15:13 NIV

MY BROTHERS AND SISTERS never give up because of the obstacles, tests, trials or tribulations that may come your way. Our God never puts more on us than we can bear. He uses His strong soldiers to accomplish His Perfect and Divine Will. So please know that it is never too late for any of us to accomplish all the desires that we may have. Please know that everything our God has planted in us shall take root and come to fruition in the on time name of Jesus.

CHAPTER THIRTEEN

SHARING THE FRUITS AND GIFTS OF THE SPIRIT WITH OTHERS

We must continue to strive daily to be a people that produce the fruits of our God's Spirit. We have been afforded the royal opportunity to do so because of His Son and our Savior Jesus Christ. As our natural fruits grow and mature they developed a sweeter taste to them. So it is with us as Christians, when we grow and mature becoming more Christ like, we too shall be as a sweet savor to God and the Body of Christ. As we continue to allow our God's root to grow up in us, we stay nourished and have the ability to nurture others.

I am the vine, you are the branches. He who abides in Me, and I in him, bears much fruit; for without Me you can do nothing.
John 15:5 NKJV

LIVE BY AND FOR THE SPIRIT OF GOD

You my brothers and sisters were called to be free. But do not use your freedom to indulge the flesh; rather serve one another humbly in love. For the entire law is fulfilled in keeping this one command: "Love your neighbor as yourself." If you bite and devour each other, watch out or we will be destroyed by each other. So I say, walk by the Spirit and you will not gratify the desires of the flesh. For the flesh desires what is contrary to the Spirit and the Spirit what is contrary to the flesh. They are in conflict with each other, so that you are not to do whatever you want. But if you are led by the Spirit you are not under the law. The acts of the flesh are obvious: sexual immorality, impurity and debauchery; idolatry and witchcraft; hatred, discord, jealousy, fits of rage, selfish ambition, dissensions, factions and envy; drunkenness, orgies, and the like. I warn you, as I did before, that those who live like this will not inherit the kingdom of God.

But the fruit of the Spirit is love, joy, peace, forbearance, kindness, goodness, faithfulness, gentleness and self- control. Against such things there is no law. Those who belong to Christ Jesus have crucified the flesh with its passions and desires. Since we live by the Spirit let us keep in step with the Spirit. Let us not become conceited, provoking and envying each other.
Galatians 5:13-26 NIV

MY BROTHERS AND SISTERS PLEASE ALLOW THE FRUIT OF OUR GOD'S SPIRIT TO TAKE ROOT IN OUR LIVES

For the fruit of the Spirit is in all goodness, righteousness and truth.
Ephesians 5:9 NKJV

To demonstrate the fruitfulness of God, we must be filled with the fruits of His Spirit. The word of our God says:

A good tree cannot bear bad fruit, nor can a bad tree bear good fruit.
Matthew 7:18 NKJV

Every branch in Me that does not bear fruit, He takes away; and every branch that bears fruit, He prunes, that it may bear more fruit.
John 15:2 NKJV

I am the vine, you are the branches. He who abides in Me, and I in Him, bears much fruit; for without Me you can do nothing.
John 15:5 NKJV

You did not choose Me, but I chose you and appointed you that you should go and bear fruit, and that your fruit should remain, that whatever you ask the Father in My name He may give you.
John 15:16 NKJV

WHEN THE SPIRIT OF GOD DWELLS WITHIN US WE ARE BLESSED TO HAVE THE FRUITS OF HIS DIVINE AND ANOINTED SPIRIT

CHAPTER FOURTEEN

THE GIFT OF LOVE

A gift has to be given by a giver. God is the giver of every good and perfect gift. The greatest gift given to us is eternal life:

For the wages of sin is death, but the gift of God is eternal life in Christ Jesus our Lord.
Romans 6:23 NKJV

My brothers and sisters, please remember that the ultimate gift is Jesus Christ, and God promises us that if we follow the ways and teachings of His Son, Jesus, we would have everything we needed.

For God so loved the world that He gave His only begotten Son, that whoever believes in Him should not perish but have everlasting life. For God did not send His Son into the world to condemn the world, but that the world, through him, might
be saved.
John 3:16-17 NKJV

Now that's some true love. The ultimate gift of God and His love has been given to us all. I love everybody and I need for you to embrace this truth: "Our positive powers outweigh, and are far greater than, any negative force."

It is so much easier to love than to hate. Just know that love heals and covers a multitude of sins. The very breath of God is what's keeping us alive this very moment. That is why we should love our God unconditionally, as well as others. We may lose our materialistic things but we will never lose the Love of God. God continue to breathe your breath of Life, Love, Joy and Peace on all of us in the Loving and On Time Name of Jesus.

The gift of love was not put in our hearts to stay. True love is not love until someone else can really feel it. Fathers, mothers, family and friends may love us, but there is no love greater than the love of God. It pleases God very much when He sees us pouring out our love to one another. When we do that it makes the world a much better place to live. Let us find that old path and walk therein, the wonderful path of peace and unconditional love.

Now that our God has placed His gift of unconditional love, and all His other gifts in our hearts, we are now anointed to share our gifts and be a true blessing to the Body of Christ.

WHAT A JOY IT IS TO RECEIVE OUR GOD'S WONDERFUL GIFTS IN THE HOLY NAME OF JESUS

To one there is given through the Spirit a message of wisdom; to another, a message of knowledge by means of the same Spirit; to another, faith by the same Spirit; to another, gifts of healing by that one Spirit; to another, miraculous powers; to another, prophecy; to another, distinguishing between Spirits; to another, speaking in different kinds of tongues; and to still another, the interpretation of tongues.
1 Corinthians 12: 8-10 NIV -

We must stay focused on our purpose and mission pertaining to the things of God. There is so much power in being obedient to the Will of God. We cannot allow anything to disturb us, nor jeopardize the joy and peace that God has placed in our hearts and minds. Our God has blessed us all with a Divine Assignment to be fulfilled in this life. So please, let's get ourselves prepared to walk in our divine purpose, knowing that our Lord and Savior Jesus Christ sacrificed His life and prepared the way for us over 2,000 years ago.

Then He said to them, "Go your way, eat the fat, drink the sweet, and send portions to those for whom nothing is prepared; for this day is holy to our Lord. Do not sorrow, for the joy of the Lord is your strength."
Nehemiah 8:10 NKJV

We serve and worship a God who is beyond awesome. There is no one word that can really define our God. I like to refer to Him as Divine Majesty. He alone holds the time to everything. God's love has been with us since the beginning of time. Our God's love is so powerful and unique that when we were disobedient in the Garden of Eden, His love did not leave us. God prepared a body for His Son, Jesus Christ, so that He could come down on earth, experience life in human form and redeem mankind back to Him. It behooves us to know where true love comes from. And if our associates or love ones are not operating in unconditional love, then we must continue to love them, but from a distance, and put them in the hands of the Lord. Our God's Love will sustain and heal us; His Divine Love is Unconditional and Everlasting. And because His Divine Love has been placed in us, many nations shall be healed. Now that we have experienced what true love really is, we can truly say, "I count it all joy, and on Christ the solid rock I stand.

But as it is written, Eye hath not seen, nor ear heard, neither have entered into the heart of man, the things which God hath prepared for them that love him
1 Corinthians 2:9 KJV

God we thank you for the gift of Your Son Jesus Christ, and for the many gifts you've blessed us all with. We are truly blessed because of the heart of Jesus Christ, who hung, bled and died on the cross for all of us.

I do not hide your righteousness in my heart; I speak of your faithfulness and salvation. I do not conceal your love and your truth from the great assembly.
Psalm 40:10 NIV

But I Am like an olive tree flourishing in the house of God; I trust in God's unfailing love for ever and ever.
Psalm 52:8 NIV

Our God sent His only begotten son from the heights of heaven just to save us. And He has given us the power and the ability to rebuke any demonic force that tries to hinder us in any way. I thank our God for His Divine love and faithfulness towards us in the awesome and on time name of Jesus

Love the Lord your God with all your heart and with all your soul and with your mind and with all your strength. The second is this: "Love your neighbor as yourself." There is no commandment greater than these.
Mark 12:30-31 NIV

But I say to you, love your enemies, bless those who curse you, do good to those who hate you, and pray for those who spitefully use you and persecute you.
Matthew 5:44 NKJV

My brothers and sisters please know that we do not have the strength to love one another on our own; we must be filled with the Spirit of God to be able to love those who have hurt us. The Word of God says:

"I can do all things through Christ who strengthens me."
Philippians 4:13 NKJV

Though I speak with the tongues of men and of angels, but have not love, I have become sounding brass or a clanging cymbal. And though I have the gift of prophecy, and understand all mysteries and all knowledge, and though I have all faith, so that I could remove mountains, but have not love, I am nothing. And though I bestow all my goods to feed the poor, and though I give my body to be burned, but have not love, it profits me nothing.

Love suffers long and is kind; love does not envy; love does not parade itself, is not puffed up; does not behave rudely, does not seek its own, is not provoked, thinks no evil; does not rejoice in iniquity, but rejoices in the truth; bears all things, believes all things, hopes all things, endures all things.

Love never fails. But whether there are prophecies, they will fail; whether there are tongues, they will cease; whether there is knowledge, it will vanish away. For we know in part and we prophesy in part. But when that which is perfect has come then that which is in part will be done away.

When I was a child, I spoke as a child, I understood as a child, I thought as a child; but when I became a man, I put away childish things. For now we see in a mirror, dimly, but then face to face. Now I know in part, but then I shall know just as I also am known.
And now abide faith, hope, love, these three; but the greatest of these is love.
1 Corinthians 13:1-13 NKJV

I beseech you therefore, brethren, by the mercies of God, that you present your bodies a living sacrifice, holy, acceptable to God, which is your reasonable service. And do not be conformed to this world, but be transformed by the renewing of your mind, that you may prove what is that good and acceptable and perfect will of God.
Romans 12:1-2 NKJV

We have now been transformed, built up, redesigned with a stronger foundation for the greater work of our God. And because of our new transformation, we should no longer second guess or question God with: But God, why am I not married yet? But God, how is it going to happen? But God, I don't see any way. But God, I have no money for this project. But God, I don't look like the rest. The "but's" can go on and on. But at this time in our lives we must move our butts (behinds) out of the way so that we may receive, and experience, the increase of our God's miraculous blessings in a greater way and on a higher level. Remember that we are filled up with our God's anointing, which shall be an overflowing source for others.

Therefore, if anyone is in Christ, he is a new creation; old things have passed away; behold, all things are become new.
2 Corinthians 5:17 NKJV

THEN GOD, OUR GOD, SAYS:

For I know the thoughts that I think toward you, saith the LORD, thoughts of peace, and not of evil, to give you an expected end.
Jeremiah 29:11 KJV

The Lord shall open to you His good treasure, the heavens, to give the rain to your land in its season, and to bless all the work of your hand. You shall lend to many nations, but you shall not borrow. And the Lord will make you the head and not the tail; you shall be above only, and not be beneath, if you heed the commandments of the Lord your God, which I command you today, and are careful to observe them. So you shall not turn aside from any of the words which I command you this day, to the right or the left, to go after other gods to serve them.
Deuteronomy 28:12-14 NKJV

And let the beauty of the Lord our God be upon us, and establish thou the work of our hands upon us; Yes, establish the work of our hands.
Psalms 90:17 NKJV

THAT EVIL SPIRIT WAS TRYING TO DESTROY MY MIND SO THAT THIS BOOK AND MANY OTHERS WOULD NOT COME INTO FRUITION.

When I look back over my life it was by God's Grace and Mercy that saved and kept me through seen and unseen dangers. I have endured a lot of pain, cried many tears, and have enough of life's scars and bruises yet my soul rejoices and still says halleluiah, because My God has brought me a mighty long way. I now know that our God allowed me to go through because He knew I could be trusted to handle all those test, trials, tribulations and fiery darts and not give up. I am so thankful for The I Am that resides inside of me. Please know that our God can and shall do the same for all who believe, have faith and trust that nothing is too hard for our God. I thank Him so much for His Perfect Divine Order in the miraculous name of Jesus.

I THANK GOD FOR THE MIND OF JESUS CHRIST!

Let this mind be in you, which was also in Christ Jesus.
Philippians 2:5 NKJV

THE EXPRESSIONS OF LOVE TO THE AUTHOR

To my first born Rev. Almeta Rhonda Bowman, the apple doesn't fall to far from the tree; you have my strength and your mother's wisdom. I see so much of the great qualities of your mother in you. You have always been a very wise and loving person I have watched you over the years, go through many challenges in life as a young person, yet you've never given up. I've been blessed to see you mature into a very powerful, strong, God fearing women that's filled with The Holy Spirit and so much Unconditional Love in your heart for others. You enrich many lives and I am very proud of you. My prayer for you is that God continues to bless, keep and guide you towards the Love of mankind and in the end you shall have joy and peace.

Always Love Your Daddy
Deacon William Thomas Bowman

So what can we say about our mother Almeta Bowman when we my brother's and myself we're growing up life wasn't always the best. We had a single mother who was trying to do her best to raise us three growing boys who by the way turned out to be three amazing men. She dropped out of school to take care of us and then went back as she got older to get her High School Diploma. She then went on to Theology School and received her Bachelor's

Degree Of Divinity. She Is an Ordained Minister and has now written her first inspiring book that is a must read.

We hope you enjoy it.

Your Sons
Alpheus Bowman, Arthur Plummer, Anwar Bowman

This is for Almeta who is my first cousin but more like a big sister to me. She is always there to give me good advice whenever I need it and she always reminds me that everything is in Divine Order. This book is a must read, after your read it you will fully understand the meaning of the phrase Divine Order.

I love you Almeta and may God Bless you and this book in a mighty way.

Yours Truly Your Cuz
John Bowman (DJ Kool)

Mommie I know you have so many people who have expressions of love... that you would need a book just to house them all...you are an amazing and anointed woman of God... whatever you need will come to you because you are correctly lined up with God, so increase has no choice but to come to you...in every area of your life...may God continue to use you to encourage His people as they are positioned/propelled for their own destinies.

Words of encouragement to my destiny Mommie, God ordains relationships...He places each of us in a position to be taught and nurtured by another to propel us into our destiny ...you have been that person to me...one who believed in me when I was too broken to believe in myself...I am truly thankful to God for His choice because it has enriched me Greatly.

Always Love Your Spiritual Daughter
Darlene Ivory

I have known Mother Queen (Almeta), My Sister in Christ, My True Friend for twenty seven (27) years; she is a phenomenal woman. Despite her own dilemma throughout her life she always gave of herself to have a listening ear and a heartfelt spirit. When she smiles you can see the anointing radiate through her. When she speaks it's like a clam stream of fresh water flowing, when she stumbled, and cried you never heard her complain or be judgmental or say a negative word, she still gave her all in helping, caring and praying for others.

This woman of God is still here for my family and me, her family, church family and so many others. She is not afraid of the true Gospel and she lets it be known. She has touched and saved hundreds of souls, I am one of them; she is always speaking and teaching the true gospel with her unique spirit and by the power of The Holy Spirit she is still touching and healing the lives of others. Can you just imagine touching and agreeing helps to spread the un-adultery gospel? She has brought me through many hard trails, tribulation and storms with the help from the Lord. When the enemy came in like the flood she was and is still here with encouraging words, her wisdom surpasses all understanding.

I have watched the years go by, God continues to take Almeta to the next level in her life, her walk with God can only take her higher and higher. Many years ago she said to me, be still, be obedient , be humble, listen, Eat God's words daily, lean not to your understanding but to God, she would say my ways are not God's ways and my thoughts are not God's thoughts; my will is not God's will, and last seek his face. Those words and encouragement has carried me through my life's struggles and now I know.

Thank you God for placing Almeta in my life (all our lives whom has been touch by her amazing grace sent from God). Almeta is like the solid rock in which she stands Heavenly

Father, thank you for keeping her from sinking sand.

All My Love Your Sister in Christ
Gwendolyn Jackson

Rev. Almeta Bowman has been my friend for over 30 years. We met in DC and everywhere she moved my family and I seemed to be in the same area in Virginia. She always appears when I'm in trouble without me even calling. Rev. Almeta has been a great asset to my family. Whenever I needed my hair, nails or feet done she would always squeeze me in. She's my riding buddy, supported me as a teacher in Fairfax county Public Schools, and in my entire church endeavors. She is a true friend, an earthly Angel, a gift sent by God who loves and cares about everyone.

Hebrews 13:2 -KJV - Be not forgetful to entertain strangers: for thereby some have entertained angels unawares

Sister in Christ
Evangelist Debra Frye

It is both an honor and a pleasure for me to greet my dear friend of nearly 20 years as she embarks upon her journey of writing about her life experiences. She has worn several hats throughout her lifetime. As a mother of 3 sons, 8 grandchildren, and three great-granddaughters, she is an expert in child rearing. Although she had sons and I had daughters, she assisted me with my girls when they were teens and both are fine adults, married, with careers and families of their own. Additionally, she has allowed my husband and me to adopt her youngest son and his family as if they were our own.

Rev. Mother Queen Almeta, as she is so affectionately referred to has served in several capacities. Not only has she been a counselor, but she serves as a mediator, too. I remain continually amazed at her innate ability to draw facts and find workable conclusions that is amicable to all parties within a finite time frame.

Rev. Almeta R. Bowman is a hard worker with a "can do" attitude. She is intelligent, professional, personable, and as we would say in the military, she is "someone that I would go to war with." I look forward to her first novel and the ones to come. As I know it will be an amazing story honoring Jesus, our Lord and Savior.

Dr. Anya Locked-Evans, MD

I have known Sister Bowman over 20 years and she has always been a loving, caring and sharing person. She has always been willing to help and assist a person in whatever goal they had. She always has a smile on her face, an encouraging word to lift your spirits. She will always have a special place in my heart for going to the funeral home and doing my Mother's hair when she transitioned to be with God. She is surely one of Gods angels.

Sincerely,
Carolyn T. Garrison

To My Daughter in Christ Rev. Almeta Bowman,

I thank God for your devoted love and friendship. Thank you for your prayers for me and my family and your understanding in times of controversy. May Gods love continue to Bless and surround you.

Yours in Christ
God Mother
Elizabeth Williamson

I met my sister in Christ, Rev. Almeta Bowman just before I was to leave going to Jerusalem. She blessed my hand, feet and gave me a massage with her anointed lotions and oils. She agreed to take care of my husband Albert while I was gone, he just had a major stoke at the time. Almeta told me that God was going to bless me in a mighty way and He surely did. My trip was truly a blessing and when I returned home I was blessed even the more. My sister in Christ you are one anointed, kind hearted, giving, loving, caring, peaceful, knowledgeable, full of wisdom, very talented, extremely creative and most of all a God fearing, virtuous women. Our spiritual relationship has grown stronger over the years. Praise is unto God for the sisterhood connection. My sister I pray that God blesses you with all of your hearts desires in the name of Jesus.

    Sister in Christ
    Billie Adams

My Dear Sister in Christ, Queen Almeta, Mother, Precious and Healer are some of the names people address her as which provides a glimpse of the light that shines within and illuminates out with ever step she takes. There are very few souls that you will have the pleasure to meet and are continually blessed by knowing them. She is a true women of valor, fearless against adversity, compassion and passionate for the kingdom. She is truly anointed with multiple talents and gifts of the Spirit. I am certain that she will reap unimaginable blessings for all of her labor and faithfulness. You will truly be blessed reading the first of many books that shares her intimate connection and revelation knowledge given from Our Lord and Savior Jesus Christ

    Sincerely Your Sister,
    Lauri Evans

Rev. Almeta Bowman is a very good friend of mine. A woman that truly walks with God and His favor is on her no matter where she is or what's she's doing. She lightens up any room; she walks into and changes the atmosphere to brightness. Everywhere she goes she's spreading the Word of God, demonstrating His unconditional love and goodness to all no matter what the condition may be. Rev. Almeta is truly anointed and it can be felt by everyone she comes in contact with. Just know that God is going to bless you beyond your imagination, I love you very much

You're Sister in Christ
Wanda Smith

Hi Almeta, Sister Girl, A mighty warrior of God who has been used by God on a daily basis to give encouraging words to her friends, family, church members and the community. Her heart and great smile is amazing and is very comforting to everyone who is hurting. She loves us as Jesus would. She always lets you know to always put your faith and trust in Him and you won't go wrong. God uses her to say precious I love you and God loves you also. When she is not doing her best, she still shows love in giving, words of praise with a concerned, peaceful, joyful and loving heart.

Rev. Mother Queen Almeta Bowman may God continue to bless you in a mighty way.

Love Always,
Connie, Debra & Charlie Ward

Miss Queen adds joy, laughter and illuminates any room she enters and makes everyone feel special and calls everyone Precious. When she is not there her presence is really missed. She shares her wisdom and knowledge with everybody. Miss Queen is a great friend, confidant, but most of all She is a True Women of God.

Proverbs 31:10: KJV- Who can find a virtuous woman? For her price is far above rubies.

Miss Queen may God bless and keep you always.

Always Love
Cedric Thomas

Miss Queen has enhanced my life through her kindness, wisdom and thoughtfulness. I appreciate all that we talk about as far as things in the world, people and you have broadened my scope as to how lots of things really are. I always look forward to seeing you and when you are not here we all miss you and love you, God is love and you are a part of it.

Always Love
Wayne Studds (Cadillac Wayne)

My Expression of Almeta Bowman

God has blessed me to be in and a part of Almeta' life; we have formed a beautiful, spiritual and Holy Ghost filled fellowship as friends, sisterhood and God Sisters. I am so blessed to have her in my life and I thank God for what He is doing in her life. Almeta is so mighty fine and I thank God for connecting us together. God looks at the heart and this Precious Woman of God possess a beautiful heart and spirit. To God be the glory for the good things He has done and for the greater things He shall continue to do in her life. My Dear and Precious Bishop Glen Alonzo Staples have taught me and others that we are to love one another, as well as to respect one another. So how is that we find so much time to judge others when there is a plank in our own eyes. If we would do as the Bible instructs us, and take the time to love and pray for one another and mean it from the heart than life would be just so mighty fine. I thank God for blessing and allowing me to observe my sister in Christ Almeta, who's life reflects all of the above attributes, she finds no fault in anyone, she loves and respects everyone no matter how they treat her. I truly love her for being an anchor in my life in the name of Jesus.

You're Sister in Christ and God Sister
Marcia Welcher-Allen (MightyFine)

To Rev. Almeta Bowman also known as "Mother Queen" a women I have admired over the years. She always displays the character of a Virtuous Woman who puts God first. She is faithful, radiates true beauty and is a humble servant.

Who can find a virtuous woman? For her price is far above rubies. Proverbs 31:10 KJV

Rev. Bowman wears all of these characteristics of a true Godly Women

Sister in Christ
Elder Marsha Rosser

God Mommy you are a muscle in the kingdom of God that is consistently faithful… shows Spiritual Power and Strength to everyone you encounter. Weather, it be a smile, hug, prayer, or just your presence, God's love is shown. I've watch you closely for nearly 10 years and you are still the same. What a wonderful, kindhearted person, that would do anything to help anybody. I admire your love for God, your strong will to be steadfast unmovable always abounding in the work of the Lord. I thank God for putting you in my life, you are a pillar in my life and I am honored to be one of your God-daughters. My prayer for you is that God gives you the desire of your heart that supper seeds what your expectations could ever imagine. Lastly, I just want you to know that I love you dearly, continue showing the love of God as you do and watch God move the mountains out of the way with your faith. God knows what you're feeling when others try to sabotage your hopes, dreams and goals but you continue to show His love. God knows about those sensitive areas in your life that only He could fill for such time as this to ultimately release that special one in your life. It's being spiritual built just for you. I'm in high expectation of this next move of God in your life! Fly God Mommy Fly Like The Eagle You Are.

God Daughter
Felicia Demery (Remy)

Once when I was lost, I met a women while on my journey…though the women was alone, she seemed to be walking with someone that could help me along my way. This woman was walking with God, and to my surprise, the earthly angel had a name: "The Mother of Queens" (Rev. Almeta Bowman. Through guidance, honesty, and supervision I was able to find my way. It was through her relationship with God that I was able to find a clear path to walk upright, virtuous, and pleasing unto God. The nurturing hand and yet stern disposition reminded me of the MOTHER within my midst, feeding my soul, helping to heal old wounds, and sharing the knowledge that only wisdom could provide from an experienced teacher. I was learning, that without (whatever the lack), God is the provider...the author and finisher of our faith—a father, a friend, a husband, a savior; Learning from a women that walks with God, not by form or fashion—but by faith and the Word of God.

She is a woman whom God walks with. Rev. Mother Queen Almeta Rhonda Bowman is a woman after God's own heart.

Spiritual Daughter
Yasemin Hanah- Peterson

Rev. Almeta Bowman is a respectable citizen, who is very well liked, and sought out after in her community. She is a loving and caring mother; as well as a phenomenal grandmother. She is very witty, innovative, gifted and creative; especially in the area of her God given healing hands that has ministered to the elite as well as; the down trodden. She has proven to many her genuine loyalty. Rev. Bowman is a very wise, discerning, spirited woman, of quality. She highly, esteems INTEGRITY as her signature voice. She has counsel and fed people from all walks of life, both spiritually and naturally. The many lives that she's touched have resulted to concrete stability emotionally; as well as spiritually, that has caused families to be enlightened and enriched by the love of God that she exudes. She is to be commended as; I'm Every Woman, the delicate Queen that she is. She love's everyone and do not mind displaying that love wherever she goes; she truly has a heart for the people.

Spiritual Daughter
Crystal Greene

Almeta is the one who doesn't go too far without touching people's hearts and lives day to day. A real humanitarian who holds true empathy for everyone in sight. She hasn't had an easy life but is very strong, compassionate and has a lot of love to give to each person she comes in contact with. I always remember Almeta and stay in touch no matter where I go, ever since we met at the health food store many years ago!

Tatiana Guerrero
Holistic Coach

I want to say a few things about Almeta Bowman, affectionately called - Queen. I have had the pleasure of knowing Queen for several years and feel she is a very gracious lady. She has shown me nothing but love and respect from the very first time I met her. Queen is a very spiritual person whose love for God is shown in her day to day walk. I have never heard her have a harsh word for anyone. She is caring and compassionate to everyone she meets. I feel proud to call her 'my friend'.

I pray that God blesses her with a long and blessed life.

Your Sister In Christ
Jackie McCormick

A great book by a great women, this is a book for a person in any situation, Knowledgeable, inspiring and caring. Ms. Bowman will tell what you need to hear! This lady is truly sent by God to uplift others on our good planet.

Neighbor
Connor Woods

Reverend Mother Queen Almeta Bowman,

I just wanted to take this time and thank you for all the wonderful kingdom work and support you give in the body of Christ:). Your leadership skills and dedication to excellence in ministry while supporting and interceding for God's people will not go unnoticed. You are definitely God's angel, watchman on the wall and a pillar within the community.

Blessed
Prophetess Vonda Farmer

God Bless You Woman of God...keep on preaching and teaching His Word ....being a light in dark places...keep walking in the authority of His Word.

Thanks for helping me take a few more steps toward the goal.

Rev. Tammy Jacko

Rev. Almeta Bowman (Queen), I met her at The Temple of Praise in Washington DC our eyes met, the hearts met, and I met the most important part of her which was the pure love of God, I thank God so much for connecting the two of us. As I read the scriptures on Sunday morning she would often tell me Precious no one delivers the scriptures like you. I didn't take it arrogantly I realized that God was using the both of us. I watched her doing our service, always taking notes from the beginning to the end, always excited about the Word of God.

The Queen, with the tambourine is and always will be a powerful, wonderful and beautiful woman of God I am so glad God connected our hearts, minds and most importantly our spirits. I pray that God blesses her always.

Minister Renee Richardson.

Rev. Almeta Bowman who I honor, love and respect as Momma Queen. She is more than a minister she is a mentor, mother figure, confidant, but most of all a dear friend. I have known Rev. Bowman since 2007. She has been all the roles I have stated in my life. She administers unconditional love and respects all she meets. Rev. Bowman has a firm foundation in the Word of God, but not to the extent that she is not in touch with her fellow man, be it young or old. She participates with the Youth and Young Adult Ministries at The Temple of Praise on a consistent basis. Rev. Bowman has open her home to me in times of need. She counsels with firmness, empathy and compassion. These qualities have afforded her the nickname of "Mother Queen". Rev. Bowman would be an asset to anyone's staff or team.

Always Love Spiritual Daughter
Karen D. Brock

Mother Queen Almeta Bowman is a wonderful person. She has shown me over the years that she is a trustworthy person and easy to approach. Also, during the time I have known Mother Bowman she has been a sweet and lovable person. The impact she has made in my life has encouraged me to keep moving forward, being careful of my surroundings, use wisdom and never stop praying.

To me she is a Queen.

Co- Pastor Annette Spivey
Ruach Temple of Praise Ministries

I have been a member of the Temple of Praise DC for five years. Without hesitation I can confidently say the Rev. Almeta Bowman is to be commended for her consistency and dedication. If ever role models are needed, that time is now. Rev. Bowman is that role model and leader. Without a spoken word, her life exemplifies that of a women committed to Christ.

She was the driving force behind my wife and me finally getting married. She respectfully encouraged us to do the right thing. The only guest to show at my graduation; she gave me a journal to document my victories, which I use only for special happenings in my life. The true definition of a "Mother of a Church" would have to include the name of Rev. Almeta Bowman. I submit this short note in humility and appreciate being able to speak on behalf of such a wonderful woman.

Respectfully submitted,
Rev. Dr. Geren Gatling
Kingdom Seekers Radio/TV Broadcast National Harbor

Mama Queen is a very humble lady and when you enter into her home she greets you with a warm smile, a big hug, and the love and kindness you feel from her is amazing. The atmosphere is so peaceful you feel welcomed and loved. And when you step in to her garden the oasis is something to behold, you experience so much happiness and joy, and to Mama Queen everyone is PRECIOUS.

I Love You Mama Queen

Sister in Christ
Cora Smart

She is more precious than rubies; her ways are pleasant ways, her paths are peace. She is truly a tree of life, a flower, a calla lily to those who take hold of her.......

Queen B is a wonderful sister in Christ. I had a chance to come to know her on 3 different occasions at the TOP church. My first time meeting her was when I walked around the church for the first time to give my offering I noticed her in the beauty of her queenish posture and her unique style. She was simply beautiful to me. My second encounter was when I went to church for holy communion on a good Friday, she was there and after I finish taking my communion, she came over and ask if I wanted her to pray for me, I said yes, she prayed and I was slayed in the spirit. So from that day forth I didn't see her as just beautiful but I saw that she was in a place in the Lord where I desired to be, she was bold, powerful and saturated in God's anointing. Everything about her to me spoke God......

I then had a chance to really get to meet her on a more personal basis, it was when she joined the dance ministry and it was there that I discovered that not only was she beautiful, bold, and powerful, but I learned that her passion for dance made her an anointed warrior who danced before the Lord, while crushing the enemy under her feet, I also learned that Queen B has a heart of gold, she loves people, she sees the best in everybody and she only speak good things, she is truly a virtuous woman of God, who lives by good example. Queen B is just a good person that loves and walks with God.

Always Love
Barbara Baylor

In the short time I have known Rev Mother Queen Almeta Bowman; she has been an encouragement to my fiancée, Catara Womack. Always exhorting and lifting up her spirit and countenance. But exhort one another daily, while it is called Today....Hebrews 3:13 KJV

Teaching and helping her with understanding.

....not in the words which man's wisdom teacheth, but which the Holy Ghost teacheth; comparing spiritual things with spiritual. I Corinthian 2:13 KJV. I thank you for your kind words to her. May the bond that you have established, the Sisterhood in Christ Jesus, blossom and grow.

Most of all may the Lord bless and keep you in all your endeavors.

Peace and happiness.
Vernon L Vassar and Catara Womack

There is so much to say about a lady that has all the credentials that Reverend Almeta Bowman has but to make it short and sweet you have to know her. Reverend Bowman is a Teacher, Mother, Grandmother, Entrepreneur, Hair Stylist and a Life Coach among many other things.

Just being in her present will lift you up if you are down. This woman of God has found her true place in life which is something most of us is still searching for. If you are in need of any service — From the Cradle to the Grave and everything in between she will be there for you. Funeral Service—Wedding Service—Baby Christening—Marriage Counseling...Or just need someone to talk too. I Myself being a Dr. of Metaphysics know that when there is a need in life—It will be met. Low and behold when my mother made her transition— Reverend Bowman appeared and did a beautiful job with the service without asking and everyone was happy. No words are great enough to thank her for what she is...An Angel of God's Universe

Dr. Nathaniel Caine (Dr. of Metaphysics) Nate the Great!

To a woman of God, all I can say about this woman of God Reverend Queen Almeta Bowman is that there is peace all around her. She is easy to talk to, makes you feel she cares, is concerned, considerate and will give you the word of God. Prayer warrior who will be there for you rest assured you will have someone that can get a prayer through.

Sister Caryl Hawkins

Miss Queen has a very caring, loving and sweet Spirit. She is full of joy and laughter, she's just a wonderful person and a blessing to all she come in Contact with. May God always bless you in Jesus Name.

God Bless
Philip Wilson

"Mother Queen"

You are such a beautiful women Ms. Lady, Proverbs 31:10 is the scripture for you. My friend…So Lovely and always loved.

Rev. Almeta Bowman (Mother Queen) is clothed with strength and dignity. She speaks with wisdom and faithful instructions are on her tongue. She is also a woman who fears the Lord and demonstrates God's love to me and others. I believe she possess true beauty which is a reflection of her soul. It is the caring that she lovingly gives and the passion that she shows to others as well as me. Mother Queen has encouraged my walk with the Lord. I appreciate her with all my heart. I extend my deepest thanks to you for all your prayers, words of encouragements, and for being my friend. You walk amongst the people like Jesus did in the Bible days. "Oh" and a special thank you to God for a special gift of a wonderful friend like you. For this very reason I am forever grateful and honored to be your friend. With each new day may peace find a place in your heart and may a full reward be given to you by God. "I truly love you for real"

With A Grateful Heart
Linda Page

We are blessed to count you as a friend and honor you as a great woman of God. You've shown us what a person can do by dedicated, faithful, and loyal service, with a determination to stay in the will of God. We rejoice with you. Many happy years ahead. Wishing you all the best, much and continued success!

God Bless You
Deacon Shawn Brickhouse

I thank God for Reverend Mother Queen Almeta! God gave me the pleasure of meeting her in line at a grocery store in Fort Washington Maryland many years ago. It was a divine encounter our spirits connected and we have been friends ever since. She is full of wisdom, peace, and most of all God's love! Each time I'm to talk with her I receive a word from the Lord or a nugget of wisdom to help me through difficult times. I thank God for allowing me to sit under such a virtuous woman in His kingdom, this woman of God also has a beautiful and loving spirit. I think of this scripture when I think of her.

Proverbs 31:26 "She openeth her mouth with wisdom; and in her tongue is the law of kindness".

Minister Cassandra Bennett
CEO & Founder of Instruments of Praise Music Institute

Mother Queen I have the utmost respect and love for you. Your kindness is always displayed and it blesses me every time I come in The Temple of Praise. I look forward to your presence. When I was sad you gave me you hand and the glory of God was radiating from you allowing me to heal. I thank God for our sister ship and for blessing me to grow as I watch you. I pray for God to always bless you.

Love,
Natasha Rochelle Conway

This little note to my sweet cousin Queen Almeta, She is very gifted in many things; I especially love her homemade lotions that smell so divine. She is a God Fearing Woman who is on FIRE FOR THE LORD. GOD has great things waiting for her, because of her obedience and faithfulness. I love you for your sweet and kind ways. Queen Almeta you must Get Ready, Get Ready for your many Blessings.

Always Love Cousin,
Darlene Murphy

I first came to know Rev. Bowman, lovingly known as Mother Queen at The Temple of Praise Church in Washington, DC. From the onset of our introduction, she has been very kind, loving and gentle to all of whom she comes in contact with. Her ability to show the love of Christ is an amazing thing to witness. She is consistently consistent in how she treats and responds to people around her, and that's always with a smile, kiss and a hug. Each Sunday, I look forward to seeing her seated at the end of the third row pew because I know that I am guaranteed a kiss and a hello Precious. She is the epitome of the kind of qualities God demands from all of us, and I'm grateful to say that I know and love her dearly.

Pastor Zina Pierre
Zina Pierre Ministries

An Ambassador of God, Queen Almeta is a woman full of wisdom, mixed with meekness and a humble heart. When I think of the Queen, I'm reminded of Matthew 10:16, "Therefore be wise as serpents and harmless as a dove", what a wonderful gift to possess.

Dr. Jewel P. Gorham

AFTERWORD

If you are where you are in life based on your decisions, then Almeta Bowman (better known as Miss Queen) has made decisions in her life that have positioned her, to put the outcomes in writing. If you can testify without a test, then Miss Queen has been and continues to be tested, and the results and knowledge gained from those test, trials, tribulations, and challenges are also in this book. If all we have to do for evil to prevail, is for good to stand by and allow it to happen.

Miss Bowman's book will move you to think and hopefully take actions in your life and the lives of others. This book was written by a woman who is a "work in progress" for those who are also "works in progress." It may never be read by "everyone," but there are words in it for "Everybody." Miss Queen's faith and tenacity has allowed her to be prepared, to anticipate, endure, survive, and to stand when the circumstances of life confronted her. This book is her testimonial. Miss Queen -- when near or far -- brings relief, comfort, wisdom, happiness, and that infectious smile speaks for itself. Her words will bring that to you, your heart, and your mind too.

Paulette Young
God Sister in Christ and Treasured Friend

CLOSING PRAYER

Father God in the name of Jesus we ask that you bless all of us. Please remove those demonic forces that try to hinder anything that needs to come forth for you. Please continue to saturate and anoint us with Your Divine Holy Spirit. God we thank you so much for allowing us to go through our test, trails and tribulation because it has truly helped to build our character. We also thank you for Your Divine and Unconditional Love. God we are most grateful to you for allowing Your Son Jesus Christ to step in on our behalf that we might have a right to eternal life. God you have made us more than conqueror's and Your Word teaches us that no weapon formed against a child shall prosper and vengeance is mine thus saith the Lord. Greater is He that is in me than he that is in the world. We can and will do all things through Christ who strengthens us. No matter what we may have to endure in this life, we will be determined to follow the teachings of our Lord and Savior Jesus Christ. We now know that following Jesus Christ shall increase our faith and bless us with the power we need to go forward. God we thank you so much for caring and bringing us through even though we do not deserve it. Father God we are so grateful to you for providing us with that sacred and secret place called The Sanctuary Within. Now God, please keep our minds focused on you so that we may continue to do Your Perfect and Divine Will here on earth.

God with great joy we shall love, worship, praise, honor and adore you for as long as we have breath in our bodies. God we ask you now to seal this pray in the Loving, Peaceful and On Time Name of Your Son and Our Savior Jesus Christ Amen. My Brothers and Sisters I Sincerely Hope That You Have Enjoyed the Journey on Finding The Sanctuary Within. I Have Asked God to bless all of us as He Showers us with an Abundance of His Unconditional Love, Joy and Peace in Our Spirits. We must continue to unconditionally love others as our God loves us, which in itself is enough to change the whole world. My brothers and sisters please continue to live in the light and be transparent for our God and through our graceful walk others will see the light of God within us.

I pray that Finding the Sanctuary Within has given all of us a greater outlook of one's self as well as life in the Awesome and Powerful Name Of Jesus Christ.

MY BROTHERS AND SISTERS PLEASE KNOW THAT OUR GOD SHALL OPEN UP THE WINDOWS OF HEAVEN AND POUR US OUT A BLESSING THAT WE SHALL NOT HAVE ROOM ENOUGH TO RECEIVE IN THE SWEET, LOVING AND WONDERFUL NAME OF OUR LORD AND SAVIOR JESUS CHRIST.

ABOUT THE AUTHOR

Almeta Rhonda Bowman is the daughter of William and the late Gloria Bowman. She is the oldest of four siblings and is a native of Washington, DC. She was raised in a loving and Christian environment. She is a mother of three sons, two daughter-in-law's, three grandsons, four granddaughters, and three great granddaughters. Life was not always easy for her, but today she stands in the victory of God, who kept her through the many seen and unseen dangers. She never shared a lot about herself to others because she always had a complex about being short and never fitting in. But today she is as a great leader, her spiritual stature is very tall, she's a nurturer and child of God who loves to follow the ways and teachings of Jesus Christ. She is very respectful, personable, courageous, caring, loving, kind, very supportive, gifted and knowledgeable about a lot of things. She's very straight forward but always in a tactful manner and she takes great responsibility for her actions.

For many years she's held several positions in Church as Sunday school and bible study teacher, pastor aid president, assistant life enrichment ministry leader, assistant women ministry leader, usher board chairperson, missionary president, women's ministry president, youth ministry coordinator, and secretary in the music ministry. She's worked and volunteered her services as a RST Bereavement Counselor (resolve through sharing) and counseled many soldiers and their families, at the Department of Ministry & Pastoral Care at Dewitt Army Community Hospital Fort Belvoir, VA. She holds a Bachelors Degree of Divinity from the Wilbur H. Waters School of Religion & Theological Seminary, Inc. Washington, DC. She is an ordained minister and substitute teacher for the Prince George County MD

School Board. Reverend Mother Queen Almeta Rhonda Bowman Is an Inspirational Speaker, Counselor And Motivator. She is a member of The Temple of Praise Washington DC under the dynamic leadership of Bishop Glen Alonzo Staples. Her life's motto is "I have been saved by grace, and kept through God's mercy." She firmly believes that no weapon formed against a child of God shall prosper and greater is He that is within me then he that is in the world. She stands on her favorite passage of scripture: Proverbs 3:5-6 "Trust in the Lord with all thine heart and lean not unto thine own understanding, but in all thy ways acknowledge him and he shall direct thy path."

Brethren, if any of you do err from the truth, and one convert him; Let him know, that he which converteth the sinner from the error of his way shall save a soul from death, and shall hide a multitude of sins
James 5:19-20 KJV

MAY OUR LIFE FLOW AS SMOOTH AND BEAUTIFUL AS A NEVER ENDING FLOW OF WATER IN THE MOST POWERFUL NAME OF OUR LORD AND SAVIOR JESUS CHRIST.

For the LORD your God is bringing you into a good land – a land with streams and pools of water, with springs flowing in the valleys and hills.
Deuteronomy 8:7

IT IS MY GREATEST DESIRE FOR ALL OF US TO LIVE A LIFE THAT IS PLEASING TO GOD THAT WOULD CAUSE OTHERS TO MAKE A CHANGE FOR THE BETTER IN THEIR LIVES, AS THEY FOLLOW THE WAYS AND TEACHINGS OF OUR LORD AND SAVIOR JESUS CHRIST.

GOD WE THANK YOU SO VERY MUCH FOR CREATING THIS SACRED SPACE IN OUR HEARTS WHERE WE ARE ALWAYS

CONNECTED TO YOU. IT HAS TRULY BEEN AN ABSOLUTE JOY FINDING THE SANCTUARY WITHIN.

God please continue to bless all of us with an abundance of spiritual understanding, more love and peace for one another that we may worship and praise you in the spirit of great unity. My brothers and sisters please know that when we are called by God, the enemy will always come at us. But all thanks is unto God for giving us that rebuking and praising power that shall ward off any demonic force that tries to attack the Sanctuary Within.

For God hath not given us the spirit of fear; but of power, and of love, and of a sound mind.
2 Timothy 1:7 (KJV)

PLEASE BE ASSURED THAT, IF WE FOLLOW THE TEACHINGS OF OUR GOD'S WORD WE SHALL BECOME A POWERFUL, POSITIVE SOURCE IN THE UNIVERSE IN THE MIRACULOUS, HEALING AND ON TIME NAME OF JESUS.

By whom also we have access by faith into this grace wherein we stand, and rejoice in hope of the glory of God.
Romans 5:2 KJV

Then they that feared the Lord spake often one to another: and the Lord hearkened, and heard it, and a book of remembrance was written before him for them that feared the Lord, and that thought upon his name. And they shall be mine, saith the Lord of hosts, in that day when I make up my jewels; and I will spare them, as a man spareth his own son that serveth him.
Malachi 3:16-17 (KJV)

FINDING THE SANCTUARY WITHIN JOURNAL TO KEEP YOUR THOUGHTS

Now, it is time for us to allow God to sit in the sanctuary of our hearts, where the Hand of God directs us to the cross; where the environment is peaceful, and conducive for Him to minister to our spirits. Let us focus our minds and worship Him as we journal our special thoughts on "Finding the Sanctuary Within". In the miraculous and on time Name of Jesus Christ.

My brothers and sisters my prayer is that our God would continuously bless all of us abundantly, with His Divine Favor, unconditional love, joy, peace, forgiving hearts, understanding and wisdom in the Anointed and Providing Name of Our Lord and Savior Jesus Christ.

Please remember that the Bible is our daily source of staying connected to the Holy Spirit, His Divine Love, and The Sanctuary Within.

RELAX, TAKE TIME TO EXPRESS WHAT YOU FEEL

LIFE IS WHAT WE MAKE IT
WHAT CHOICE WOULD I MAKE FOR MY LIFE?

That thou stir up the gift of God, which is in thee by the putting on of my hands.
2 Timothy 1:6 KJV

EXPRESS THE BEAUTY OF GOD WITHIN YOU

ALLOW THE HOLY SPIRIT TO LEAD YOUR LIFE

I AM REALLY ENJOYING GOD'S UNCONDITIONAL LOVE, JOY AND PEACE IN MY LIFE.

GOD I KNOW THAT YOUR FAITH WILL CARRY ME THROUGH

THE LORD IS MY PROVIDER OF EVERYTHING AND I SHALL NOT WANT FOR ANYTHING

I WILL CONTINUE TO TRUST GOD WITH MY WHOLE HEART

For I will pour water on the thirsty land, and streams on the dry ground; I will pour out my spirit on your offspring, and my blessing on your descendants
Isaiah 44:3 KJV

ALL BEAUTIFUL THINGS GROW WITH GOD'S LOVE

GOD PLEASE BLESS ME TO BE A DIVINE INSTRUMENT OF YOUR LIGHT

DAILY AFFIRMATIONS OF THE SCRIPTURES

Jesus came and made the way possible for me.

God, your path is the direction for my life.

God, my heart and soul says yes to Your Perfect and Divine Will.

God, I humbly thank You for creating a clean heart within me.

For whosoever will save his life shall lose it: and whosoever will lose his life for my sake shall find it.
Matthew 16:25 KJV

God I welcome your divine joy in my life.

I will bless the lord at all times: his praise shall continually be in my mouth.
Psalm 34:1

He that dwelleth in the secret place of the most high shall abide under the shadow of the almighty.
Psalm 91:1

And he that keepeth his commandments dwelleth in him, and he in him. And hereby we know that he abideth in us, by the spirit which he hath given us.
1 John 3:24

God, I need for You to speak to my heart like never before.

God, I thank You for Your Divine Grace and Mercy in the name of Jesus.

God, we thank You so very much for Your Divine Favor over our lives in the miraculous name of Jesus.

God, because of Finding the Sanctuary Within Your unconditional love can grow fruitfully in my heart.

God, I thank You for being my peace.

My destiny has purpose now, because of Finding the Sanctuary Within

I AM WONDEROUSLY BLESSED, AND I ONLY EMBRACE THE PERFECTIONS OF GOD FOR MY LIFE IN THE MIRACULOUS AND ON TIME NAME OF JESUS.

The Lord is my light and my salvation; whom shall I fear? The Lord is the strength of my life; of whom shall I be afraid?
When the wicked came against me to eat up my flesh, my enemies and foes, they stumbled and fell.
Though an army may encamp against me, my heart shall not fear; though war may rise against me, in this I will be confident.
One thing I have desired of the Lord, that will I seek:
That I may dwell in the house of the Lord all the days of my life, to behold the beauty of the Lord, and to inquire in His temple. ...
Wait on the Lord; be of good courage, and He shall strengthen your heart; wait, I say, on the Lord!
Psalm 27:1-4, 14 NKJV

> Looking unto *Jesus* the author and finisher of our faith; who for the joy that was set before him endured the cross, despising the shame, and is set down at the right hand of the throne of God.

Trusting Our God to bless you in Finding the Sanctuary Within

Always Love, Reverend Mother Queen Almeta Rhonda Bowman

Stay Connected:

Email: findingthesanctuarywithin@gmail.com
agodsangel8@gmail.com

PO Box 159
Mount Vernon, Virginia 22121

Follow me on Social Media:
Twitter (AlmetaBowman@MotherQueenA)
LinkedIn (Almeta Bowman)
Instagram (Almeta.Bowman)
Facebook (Almeta.Bowman)
You Tube (Almeta Bowman Finding the Sanctuary Within)
Myspace (Almeta Bowman)

Made in the USA
Middletown, DE
05 June 2020